Y. Q M Office
Z. c.s. Storehouse
1. Old Adjutants Office
2. C.S. Office
3. New Adjutants Office
4. Post Trader
5. Citizen Employees
6. Schoolhouse
7. Post Guides
8. Sawyers House
9. Saw Mill
10. Brickyard

11. Gardens
12. Butchershop

CAMP APACHE

A. T.

March 1877.

1000 feet

500

100

Trail to Tonto Basin

White River

WITH SCOUTS AND CAVALRY

AT

FORT APACHE

LIEUTENANT H. B. WHARFIELD, *Tenth Cavalry*

With Scouts and Cavalry

At

Fort Apache

BY

Col. H. B. Wharfield, USAF, Ret.

EDITED BY

John Alexander Carroll

Professor of History
The University of Arizona

ARIZONA PIONEERS' HISTORICAL SOCIETY

TUCSON 1965 ARIZONA

Manufactured in the United States of America

CONTENTS

ILLUSTRATIONS

A DEDICATION

and an acknowledgment

To my dear wife, MYRTLE, *and
beloved daughters,* KATHRYN
and JEANNE, *camp followers
of mine to many Army posts.*

The introduction and footnotes by Dr. John Alexander Carroll of the University of Arizona are of major importance to this publication under the imprint of the Arizona Pioneers' Historical Society. To an old cavalryman these scholarly additions bring a delight far beyond the limitations of expression within a stable or troop vocabulary. Perhaps my feelings can best be set forth in the words of the Apache scout, First Sergeant Eskehnadestah, who described a fight with Pancho Villa's forces during the Pershing Punitive Expedition of 1916 by saying, "Huli! Damn Good." Dr. Carroll is a man truly of the Western spirit and energy. As a former officer of the 10th Cavalry I would say, "He would have made a fine cavalryman."

I also wish to acknowledge the following persons for their invaluable assistance: Lieutenant Colonel John H. Healy, USA, Retired, of the cavalry and former commanding officer of the Detachment of Indian Scouts; Yndia Smalley Moore for her administrative help and assistance; Dr. Odie B. Faulk of the Arizona Pioneers' Historical Society, historian and author, who has used of his skills in the publication of this book; Orville A. Cochran, Fort Huachuca Post Historian; John W. Gross and John C. Burk of the Army Military Personnel Records Center, St. Louis; Mrs. June Larzelere Dillon, daughter of "Peasoup"; Don Carleton Cooley, Jr., grandson of ex-Army Scout Cooley; and Fred Banashley, Apache Tribal Vice-Chairman.

An

INTRODUCTION

THE MERE MENTION of the American West brings to mind many images —
conquistadors, Jesuit and Franciscan missionaries, fur trappers and traders,
cowboys and longhorns, peace officers and outlaws. Yet of all the characters
playing out their roles in this great expanse of desert and mountains, of rivers
and forests, it was perhaps the Cavalryman and the Indian who have most
dramatically caught and held the public imagination. These two frontier types,
locked in a struggle for mastery of half a continent, dominate the motion picture
and television screens; they have been the subject of a plethora of printed words,
the true-to-fact and the fictional, good and otherwise. They symbolize the West
at its best and at its worst, at its moments of greatness and of tragedy. This "last
best West" — the American frontier that has been most popularized — actually
lasted only for little more than twenty-five years. By the 1890's the free land
was gone, the beaver had been trapped, the cattle kingdom was restricted by
fences, the Indian had been reduced to reservations, and most of the military
posts had been deactivated and sold at public auction.

Yet echoes of this epoch have lingered like the haunting strains of a melody
so beautiful that it cannot be forgotten. Many of the participants in that golden
age of the West wrote of their experiences; the shelves of even the humblest
public or college library are rich with reminiscences, diaries, and twice-told
accounts of the heroic — and the commonplace — details of the era. Once the
pioneers had passed away, professional and amateur historians took up the task,
and the chronicling has continued. The spring and autumn lists of almost every
publisher carry new and reprinted titles which tell and tell again the classic story
of war whoop and saber.

What has been forgotten in this rush to retell the golden age of the West is
the fact that this period did not end at a given date. The surrender of Geronimo
did not see the disbandment of the Apache Scouts, the "eyes" of the Army in
the Southwest. The Battle of Wounded Knee did not forever break the Redman's
spirit on the Plains. The address of Frederick Jackson Turner to the American
Historical Association in 1893, wherein he stated that there was no more free
land in the West, did not stop the overland migration. No, civilization did not
spring forth in full flower on the frontier when the last warrior laid down his
weapon or when the rancher strung his barbed wire across the north side of his
land and completed enclosing it. Men continued to go west — to farm, to ranch,
to soldier, or just "to see the elephant." The romance and the lure of the West
lingered for years, a twilight period of transition in the march of "progress" and

urbanization. This is a period still alive in the memories of living men — men such as Colonel H. B. Wharfield.

Because the post-1890's was a period less glamorous than the previous quarter century in the development of the West, little has been written about it, or at least little has been published. Little is known, therefore, of the life of a cavalryman in the post-Indian War era. Colonel Wharfield has attempted to fill that gap. As a first lieutenant of cavalry, he was sent in 1918 to Fort Apache, Arizona, one of the old frontier posts from which cavalry units had gone out in pursuit of restless Apache warriors. It took Wharfield a two-day horseback ride to reach the fort, which was connected with the outside world only by means of a telegraph line and a wagon train that freighted in its supplies. At Fort Apache the young officer assumed command of a troop of the 10th Cavalry, the famous Negro regiment long active on the Southwestern frontier under Colonel B. H. Grierson, and a detachment of Indian Scouts, originally organized by General George Crook and active in the Apache wars.

At that time the post was relatively unimportant in the mainstream of Arizona history. Books chronicling that era, even those few concerned primarily with the "Baby State," are filled with strange names such as Verdun and Argonne. The characters at Fort Apache played no important roles on the stage of history. Yet they lived a way of life that in itself was highly important in the larger perspectives of the American West. Thus Colonel Wharfield's story is valuable in the field of recent military history, and in the area of description rather than of chronicle. It is a convincing portrayal of the life of the cavalry near the end of its illustrious service to the republic, and it unfolds a graphic picture of conditions in one of the more primitive and remote areas of the West at a time when most Americans considered the region civilized. His story is recommended reading not only for old soldiers who have not faded away, but also for any student of the American frontier who wishes to complete his education. The 10th Cavalry and the Apache Scouts of 1918 were the heirs and descendants of Grierson, of Custer and the 7th Cavalry, of Carr and the 6th. They were Arizonans and Westerners in the finest tradition, and by stint of service they contributed to the development of the region. Most western enthusiasts, therefore, will discover that the title *With Scouts and Cavalry at Fort Apache* has not misled them from their field of interest.

JOHN ALEXANDER CARROLL
The University of Arizona
August 1965

I

ENROUTE TO THE FORT

Headquarters Tenth Cavalry
Fort Huachuca, Arizona
January 8, 1918

Special Orders)
No.   4)
    1. First Lieutenant HAROLD B. WHARFIELD *is assigned to Troop "L" stationed at Fort Apache and will join the troop to which assigned.*

By order of Major Rodney

J. F. RICHMOND
Capt. & Adjutant, 10th Cavalry, USA

When this order arrived, I was with Captain Pinckney Armstrong's Troop H, 2nd Squadron, 10th U. S. Cavalry, in camp at Nogales, Arizona. I had been in the 10th for less than six months, but already I was proud of the famous old regiment as a young officer could be. The 10th had been organized in 1866 as one of two new Negro cavalry regiments. Brevet Major General Benjamin H. Grierson, noted for his daring raid behind Confederate lines in the Civil War, was its first colonel and commanded the regiment for twenty-two years. Grierson's "Buffalo Soldiers" earned a fine reputation for service on the

[*1*]

Southern Plains and in the Southwest, and various units saw action against bands of Comanches, Kiowas, Kiowa Apaches, Mescalero Apaches, and Chiricahua Apaches. At different times during the Indian campaigns the regiment maintained headquarters at Fort Riley, Fort Sill, Fort Davis in Texas, and Whipple Barracks and Fort Grant in Arizona. During the Spanish-American War the regiment was in General Wheeler's division in Cuba and saw hard fighting as part of the 2nd Cavalry Brigade, which included Teddy Roosevelt's Rough Riders. In 1916 the 10th was with General Pershing's Punitive Expedition into Mexico in pursuit of Pancho Villa, and in that campaign Colonel DeRosey C. Cabell, now the regimental commander, was Pershing's chief of staff. The 10th U. S. Cavalry had a grand history, and I was glad to belong to it.

I did not, however, especially care to leave Captain Pinckney Armstrong's outfit. Pink, as he was companionably called, was my ideal of a border cavalryman. He was a soldier of the old school, of the same model as the frontier cavalryman in Frederic Remington's drawings, a twenty-year man of genuine toughness who had campaigned in Cuba, the Philippines, and Mexico, and had been a sergeant in the 2nd Cavalry and the 5th Cavalry before receiving a temporary commission in the National Army at the outbreak of World War I.* The

---

* Pink's service record shows that he was born in Belmont, Illinois, in 1874 and enlisted in the 2nd U. S. Cavalry in 1895, serving in this regiment until he joined the 5th U. S. Cavalry in 1905. He was commissioned a temporary captain in 1917 and assigned to the 10th U. S. Cavalry. In July of 1918 he was promoted to major and reassigned to the 62nd Pioneer Infantry, subsequently served at a port of embarkation, and then was commander of Camp Halland Alexander in Virginia. After the Armistice he was honorably discharged from his temporary commission and enlisted in the 1st U. S. Cavalry. He was stationed with a troop of the 1st Cavalry at Fort Apache, Arizona, until 1921. Upon appointment as a warrant officer in January of 1922, he was assigned to Headquarters, 9th Corps Area, at the Presidio of San Francisco, where he served until his retirement on October 21, 1926. He died at Nevada City, California, as a retired major of cavalry on September 13, 1933. At Fort Huachuca in 1919 someone gave out the information that Pink had died of pneumonia at an Army camp near Jacksonville, Florida; not until I obtained official information did I realize that he had lived on to retirement. Lieutenant Alfred J. de Lorimier, one of the shavetails of Troop H at Nogales, wrote in later years: "Pink was one of the finest

shave-tails of his Troop H believed in the old Army saying that when you are with a good C.O., don't get itchy feet for a change. Those were my sentiments. Furthermore, we were enjoying the Mexican border duty at the camps out from Nogales in the vicinity of Arivaca and Lochiel, spending our spare time hunting while patrolling for smugglers and bandits, as well as Yaqui Indians, from across the line. It was hard to imagine better duty.

Pink told me, however, that I was fortunate to get an assignment to Fort Apache. In his opinion this was the best place in Arizona for a soldier who liked to ride and hunt. Having himself served there for a number of years with the 5th Cavalry and having hunted with the Apache Indian Scouts, he was enthusiastic about what he called my good luck. Lieutenant William Scott of Troop E, which was also at Nogales, likewise had been at Fort Apache, and he added to Pink's views. He told me that the fort had been established in the seventies to control the Indians, and that General George Crook had enlisted a large number of White Mountain Apaches as scouts in his campaigns against Geronimo and the renegade Chiricahuas. Scotty had seen the present-day Apache Scouts in action in Mexico in 1916 with General Pershing's expedition after Pancho Villa, and said they could track anything even in dry country.

After those two old-time cavalrymen had given me a good briefing on Fort Apache, I became anxious to be on my way to that remote place, which was situated off the railroad some one hundred miles from Holbrook in the White Mountains of east-central Arizona. On January 25, 1918, I took the local train out of Nogales and changed at Tucson for Phoenix, where I laid over to visit the state capitol. There I renewed acquaintance with the state adjutant general and paid my respects to Governor George W. P. Hunt. The governor was a gentleman of the

men, and I'll always remember him with a lump in my throat because of the many little acts of real kindness he extended to me. . . . On a damn cold rainy night when we were bivouacked on the bleak Mexican border below Arivaca, Arizona, I awoke to find Pink's blankets over me. He had spent most of the night by himself, huddled near the camp fire. He taught me more than any other officer in the Army, not only in soldiering know-how but in loyalty and honesty and courage. May God bless his grand old soul."

old political school of the West; he was quite stout, of the age beyond his early-day, hard-muscled physique, with a walrus mustache and gold watch chain across his vest front. We had a pleasant conversation. The next day I started north for Holbrook, the railhead for Fort Apache.

Upon arriving at Holbrook in the evening, I went to the hotel to clean up. There I met a white sergeant of the Quartermaster detachment at the fort who until recently had been a cowboy with the well-known Chiricahua Cattle Company. My inquiry about military transportation brought a reply from Sergeant Meyers that the only thing available was the wagon train then loading up; but since he was taking back a bunch of the Apache Scout ponies, he suggested that I might like to go with him. The chance of riding horseback to the fort sounded good, and I accepted. The next morning I toured the town. The sergeant took me to the warehouse and office of the firm which stored the government freight. At the Merchants and Stockgrowers Bank, I met the cashier who sent the currency to the post for payment of the troops. After lunch at a restaurant run by an old Chinaman, we went over to the camp of the wagon train detail. There I met Sergeant Charles W. Larzelere, who had charge of the entire train of twenty-eight wagons with four mules each and thirty-five enlisted men. The detail was composed of white and Negro soldiers of the Quartermaster detachment, Negro troopers of the 10th Cavalry, and five Apache scouts.

Sergeant Larzelere had been in the Army for twenty years, serving in the 7th Field Artillery, the 3rd Cavalry, and a number of enlistments in the 5th Cavalry. At the present time his service with the Quartermaster Corps enabled him to remain at the fort with his Apache wife, Pauline, and family.[†] The sergeant impressed me as a good example of the finest type of non-commissioned officers in the Army.

[†] Charles W. Larzelere was born in Trenton, New Jersey, in 1880, and enlisted in the 7th Artillery during the Spanish-American War. He had served as a wagoner, cook, and corporal of cavalry before becoming a corporal in the Quartermaster Corps in 1914. He became a sergeant in 1918, a master sergeant in 1927, and retired that year. He died on July 31, 1937, and was buried in the Whiteriver Cemetery near Fort Apache. Two sons, Frank and Fred, now live in the vicinity of Whiteriver, and a daughter, Mrs. June Larzelere Dillon, resides at McNary, Arizona.

"Pink" Armstrong, left; Marcus E. Jones,
bottom left; and John C. F. Tillson,
bottom right.

Dr. Robert H. McLeod, *above left;*
Dr. J. Lee Borden, *above right;*
and *"Peasoup" Larzelere (courtesy
Mrs. June Larzelere Dillon) in
retirement, right.*

En Route to the Fort

That view never changed throughout my service with the man. A letter of commendation from an officer of the 5th Cavalry, subsequently brought to my attention, well substantiated my first impression of him. It is set out in full as worthy of record.

Fort Apache, Ariz., Oct. 31, 1913

1. When Private Charles W. Larzelere, Q.M. Corps, took charge of the pack train at this post on March 15th 1913, the whole equipment of the pack train was in a very bad condition and the mules had not had the proper care and many of them had bruised and sore backs.

2. Private Larzelere has worked faithfully and has wonderfully improved the condition of all pertaining to the pack train, his care and training of the mules is especially worthy of commendation.

3. This man would make an excellent packmaster, as he is an excellent soldier, packer, and cargadore, and would make an excellent non-commissioned officer.

Robt. M. Barton
1st. Lieut. 5th Cavalry
A.Q.M.

He was called Peasoup, the usual nickname in those times for a person of French extraction, by his Army mule-skinners. Several of the Apache scout drivers, however, could master only the English word "Soup," and that was his full name to them.

We left Holbrook late the next morning and headed south along the dusty desert road for the town of Snowflake, where it was our plan to stop for the first night. I led the way on a black Indian pony and Sergeant Meyers brought up the rear, herding a bunch of eight ponies along behind me. In mid-afternoon we came up over a rise and saw a veritable oasis in the desert. It was the old Mormon settlement of Snowflake. As we rode through the main street, several dogs made a dash at our loose stock, but we got them into the corral at the livery stable without a stampede.

A big old-fashioned house was the hotel. It was operated by a family of Mormons whose hospitality had the natural manner and grace that has made the West best known to all strangers. After arranging for our lodging, Sergeant Meyers and I walked out on the porch. It was a peaceful and quiet scene of well-being and contented community life we saw during the late afternoon in that little settlement. An occasional plain-dressed woman came along the main street with a market-basket on an arm and children following behind her. A few dogs wandered around listlessly or lay on the shady platforms in front of the few stores. Down the street a couple of huge Mormon freight wagons with trailers were unloading. Outside the livery stable corral some range cattle were milling about, trying to reach into the mangers for hay. Saddled cow-ponies were tied to the hitching rack in front of a store, heads hanging down and a hind leg hunched up in a resting position, patiently waiting for the riders to come out.

In a nearby trading store Sergeant Meyers met an old friend named Priebe, whom he knew when they both worked for the Chiricahua Cattle Company down on the Indian reservation. We walked back together to the hotel as it was nearing suppertime. As we sat around in the living room that evening, I enjoyed their talk about persons in the towns along the route and cowhands they knew with the Chiricahua outfit, and especially about their intimate knowledge of various horses. Finally the sergeant asked Priebe about the long-legged mule that was his favorite mount in working the rimrock country. He grinned self-consciously and said the mule had died. After a short silence as we waited for an explanation, he looked up and said it was an accident. Then Priebe told us a strange story.

He was working alone on the upper Tonto Creek trying to locate cows with late calves that had not been branded in the round-up. The night before he had hobbled the mule so it could graze. In the morning it was gone, and starting on foot to trail it, Priebe soon realized the signs were not hobbled jumps. Returning to camp, he got his rope and rifle and started on the trail, not waiting to get breakfast. After going a mile or so he sighted the mule grazing. As he came closer, the animal looked up and cocked its ears but did not move. Taking off his hat, Priebe held it out toward the mule and shook it as though full of oats. The animal waited and watched until he approached fairly close, then trotted off. This maneuvering was repeated a number of times, and Priebe became madder and madder. Then he tried to circle the mule and head it back toward camp, but had no luck. Finally he threw a shell into the gun and aimed for the crest of the mule's neck to crease it and knock the animal down. Just as he squeezed the trigger, the mule broke into a run, then pitched head over heels to the ground. Priebe said that he walked over to his dead mule, kicked it in the ribs, and turned back to camp. After eating a hasty breakfast there, he had a day's hike across to Bill Ryan's ranch where he got a horse.

Sergeant Meyers and I left at daybreak to cover the remaining seventy miles to Fort Apache, intending to push along and change mounts frequently. The loose ponies followed without much attention, and we both rode at the head to get out of the dust. Toward noon we came to the settlement of Show Low, and stopped there to eat and change mounts. This place was one of a number of overnight camps for the post wagon train. The camp site was not a very good place, but water was convenient. The hay and sacks of grain were stacked in a small fenced enclosure. Two large pyramidal tents furnished the teamsters some cover, and a makeshift canvas-covered shelter served for a kitchen. Grasshopper, an Apache scout, and his family were located there to protect government property, and had put up a teepee near the water hole. I stopped to talk to the scout, but he did not understand much English so I walked around the camp to make a general inspection of conditions there.

Sergeant Meyers told me that Show Low used to be the ranch head-quarters of a former Army scout by the name of Cooley and his partner. The two men had numerous disagreements, and one night they played a game of Seven-Up for the ranch. On the last hand the partner said, "Show low and you win"; and Cooley won. That card game gave the name of Show Low to the ranch, the main creek, and also to the settle-ment. Cooley married two daughters of an Apache chief. Later he sold the ranch and settled on land near the Mormon town of Pinetop, about twenty miles up the mountain. Sergeant Meyers also told me that he had known the Cooleys for a long time, and attended the burial ceremony for the old Army scout at the Fort Apache cemetery last spring. However, Molly, the surviving wife, was around and enjoyed having people stop by to talk to her.

At a little store-restaurant we got something to eat. Coming outside, Sergeant Meyers met a bushy-whiskered old cowman he had known for a long time. All of us sat on the store platform to rest and to talk. Soon I had a chance to ask if he had known the old Army scout Cooley. Shoving his hat on the back of his head and taking a long spit of a tobacco chew out into the street, the cowman said: "Dang right I knowd ol' Cooley. He done died last spring, but Molly lives up on the ol' place. Hyard lots from the ol' coot hisself 'bout comin' into this here country an' his scoutin' fer General Crook." The old man was a great talker and an entertaining storyteller. We sat there in the shade for over an hour listening to his tales of the old days when the Apaches were hostile. Many of the episodes he related concerned Cooley. Since it was necessary to leave if we wanted to make the fort that night, we finally said good-bye to the old cowboy and started the herd of ponies up the road.

Later I learned more about the history of Corydon Eliphalet Cooley and his Apache wife, Molly. Most of the writings about the Apache campaigns of General George Crook mention his scouting work and good influence over the bands of Pedro and Miguel. Cooley was born near Stauton, Virginia, in 1836 of a prominent family, and had a good education. When twenty years old, he went to Santa Fe. At one time he worked in Denver for Ceran St. Vrain, the famous mountain man and fur trader, and also as a quartermaster at Fort Craig in New Mexico.

When the Civil War started he was in Santa Fe. Along with other mountaineers, fur traders, and miners, as well as Jicarilla Apaches, he joined the Union volunteers organized to protect the region against General H. H. Sibley's invading Texans of the Confederacy. Cooley and two companions came into Arizona upon learning of fabulous "lost" gold placers which a Dr. Thorne of Lemitar, New Mexico, had seen somewhere in the White Mountains while a captive of the Apaches. It was on this fruitless trip that he was attracted to the Show Low area, where he located a ranch in the land of the Sierra Blanca Apaches.

Cooley rendered good service as a scout and interpreter for General Crook during the various Indian campaigns of 1872-1873. His last scouting for the Army was in 1882 when he and three other men accompanied Crook on a dangerous mission to the Black River ford for a talk with hostile Apache chiefs. It is reported that Cooley made his will prior to the trip because it was feared the entire party would be massacred. The general left word at the fort that if they did not return within five days a detachment could be sent to the area; but at the end of the third day the party came back.

The first Cooley ranch, at the headwaters of a tributary of Silver Creek, was held in partnership with Marion Clark, who laid claim to a creek valley in the area. It was perhaps in 1876 that the parties decided to dissolve the business arrangement in a most unconventional manner by a game of Seven-Up. Later Cooley took Henry Huning as a partner on the Show Low ranch. In 1888 he sold out and moved to a new location near the northern boundary of the Indian reservation. It was while living at the Show Low ranch that he married two daughters of Chief Pedro, a prominent leader among the Sierra Blanca bands. This was the accepted custom with the Apaches. One of the wives died during childbirth. Molly, the other wife, was a remarkable Indian woman of extraordinary character. During the various times that Cooley was on duty at Fort Apache as a scout, she tried hard to learn how the Army women did their housekeeping. They in turn were delighted to help the pretty young Indian woman learn to cook American foods, set a table, and keep house. She was also eager that her children be taught to read and write, and that they get an education.

I later knew two boys of the family. Bert Cooley, an enlisted soldier in the Quartermaster Corps at the fort, was an intelligent man and a good mechanic. Corydon, one of the older children, had a formal education and in later years owned successful businesses, one of which was a trading post at Cibecue. The Cooley name to this day is well and favorably known throughout the region. All the children and their descendants are respected citizens, and have preserved the good name of the old Army scout and his remarkable wife, Molly.

The home of the Cooleys was always open to travelers through the country, and became a favorite stop-over for Army people. Mr. Cooley had an Irishman's good humor and was a fine host with his jokes and laughter. Mrs. Cooley set the best "table" in the region with a variety of garden vegetables, fruit from the orchard, dairy products, poultry, and meat of fat beef, as well as wild game. In accounts of Cooley's hospitality, comment has always been made of the excellent home maintained by this Apache woman and her kindness to strangers, as well as praise of her accomplishments. When we pulled into the Cooley ranch, we saw Mrs. Cooley sitting in a sunny spot on the wide veranda of the large two-storied house busy hand-sewing on a garment. Sergeant Meyers previously had told me that Molly understood English perfectly, but would only respond in Apache. In the early days some officer at the fort had ridiculed and laughed at her attempts to speak the new language. That thoughtless act had so embarrassed and discouraged her that she stopped trying to speak English.

We rode over and talked for a few minutes. I told her of my transfer from Fort Huachuca and said that it was a pleasure to be in this region. She smiled and made a reply in her native language. Then she asked about Peasoup, and the sergeant understood enough Apache to reply that the wagon train would be along within a few days. He also said in a joking manner that both of us were starving and would at least like a drink of water. At that Molly laughed and, waving a hand toward the kitchen door, said that she would feed the lieutenant but Meyers was getting too fat and should not eat much. Tying up our mounts and leaving the other ponies grazing, we started around to the steps and met her son Corydon walking over from the corral. He, too, asked us to come in and have a bite to eat. As we walked toward the door he said, "Maw likes to have people stop by as she gets mighty lonesome since Father died, and not many stop nowadays. But Peasoup always rides in or shouts at her when the wagon train passes."

Before we started on the ride down the mountain toward the post, I changed mounts as my pony was showing some weariness. The animals were put into a steady trot in order to get along through the pine forests as far as possible before night. It was an hour or more past darkness when we rode through the Whiteriver Indian agency, and going right along we took a lower road for the last four miles to the fort. It seemed a long time before we saw lights. The animals splashed through the shallow crossing of the East Fork of the White River, and broke into a very fast trot as we came to the outskirts of a group of buildings. At the quartermaster corral a soldier opened the gate and said they had been expecting us. I took the boardwalk along the kerosene-lamp lighted street toward the quarters of the commanding officer to report my arrival. I was now at the old frontier post of Fort Apache.

II

FORT APACHE

IT WAS A FIVE-MINUTE WALK to the quarters of the commanding officer, Captain John C. F. Tillson, on the other side of the post.
Upon my arrival there, he opened the door and immediately invited
me inside with the word that he had been expecting me all day long
and was glad I had arrived. Mrs. Tillson came forward with a welcome, explaining that the children were in bed but could see me in
the morning. Neither had been away from the post for over two years,
and were eager for every bit of personal news I could give of Fort
Huachuca and the regiment. The conversation carried on and on for
a number of hours before any thought was given to retiring. As the
captain handed me the lamp for my room, he said that they hoped I
would be their guest at least until my quarters were arranged. That
hospitable military custom and their graciousness were appreciated, and
I remained at their home for a week until my baggage arrived on the
wagon train.

Captain Tillson was "old Army." His grandfather had fought in
the Civil War with a New York regiment; his father, then a colonel
was a graduate of West Point in 1878. The captain was born at the
old frontier post of Fort Keogh, near Miles City, Montana, in 1886
while his father was stationed there as a lieutenant in the 5th Infantry.
Captain Tillson himself had been a cadet at West Point from 1904
to 1906 when he withdrew from the Academy and enlisted in Troop L,
2nd Cavalry. By competitive examination he was appointed a second

lieutenant of cavalry in 1909, and five years later was graduated from the Mounted Service School at Fort Riley and assigned to the 10th Cavalry at Fort Huachuca. In 1916 he was promoted to first lieutenant, and the following year he advanced to the rank of captain.* As I remember him at Fort Apache, he was trim, of medium height, and carried himself as one born to the mounted service. Such a military bearing was the outward reflection of an active mind, much energy, and self-discipline.

The next day Captain Tillson instructed the first sergeant to take the troop out for exercise. Then he spent the morning showing me the post. First he took me to a stable back of the quarters to see his two private mounts. The horses were thoroughbreds which had been purchased from a race track in El Paso, Texas, and the finest officer mounts I had ever seen. We then walked along the tree-lined officers row to the old Adjutant's building at the upper end of the parade ground, where the captain went into the headquarters office to take care of necessary paperwork. I stood on the porch of the old adobe building and looked out across the four or five acres of parade ground. The post had the usual arrangement of officers' quarters on one side and the barracks for the enlisted personnel on the other side of the parade ground. At the lower end was a rambling building which I took to be the hospital. Boardwalks and a dirt road extended around the area, and old-fashioned picket fences enclosed all the yards of the quarters. On a stepladder leaning against one of the street lamp standards was a civilian cleaning the light globes and filling the kerosene lamps. At the farther end of the officers row I could make out a number of log cabins which were part of the original fort.

---

* Subsequently he served with the 7th Cavalry at Fort Bliss, at Infantry Replacement camps in Virginia and Maryland, and with the 22nd Infantry in the rank of major, National Army. In 1920 he was appointed major in the regular Army and assigned to the 12th Cavalry, and later to the 1st Cavalry. He was graduated from the advanced course of the Cavalry School in 1925, from the Command and General Staff School in 1926, and from the Army War College in 1931. He was promoted to lieutenant colonel in 1934, to colonel in 1938 while with the 5th Cavalry, and was retired for physical disability in February of 1943. He lives near Fort Sam Houston, San Antonio.

The little I had seen of Captain Tillson assured me that he was a high type of cavalry officer from whom I, as a young man, could learn much about soldiering; that subsequently proved correct. An orderly stepped out of the hallway, saluted, and said, "The Captain's compliments, Sir. The Captain would like to see the Lieutenant in his office." That was a sufficient introduction to the military morale and esprit de corps of the post to give evidence that here was a high standard military organization. As I stepped into his office, taking off my hat, I quickly came to a salute, as he rose from his chair to respond. Throughout my entire service with the captain he never failed, if seated, to stand and return the salute of an officer or enlisted man. It was not an idiosyncracy on his part, but a natural courtesy and knowledge that a salute entitled the individual to a proper response.

He handed me a post order, and said that now I was the commanding officer of the Detachment of Indian Scouts. Then he spoke about the organizations and administration here. The post, even though regimental in size, was garrisoned only by one Negro troop of the 10th Cavalry, twenty-two Apache scouts, detachments of the quartermaster corps, medical corps, signal and ordnance corps, and five civilian employees — in all, two hundred and eleven men according to the latest subsistence report. Smiling, the captain stated that he was the commanding officer of the post, troop commander, acting Quartermaster, post engineer, signal officer, post exchange officer, and, whenever the doctor was away, he also commanded the medical detachment. Doctor Robert H. McLeod of Palestine, Texas, a medical captain, and I were the only officers on his staff; and since post duties were not assigned to a doctor, it looked as though I was to have all the minor titles and all the work.

Rolling and lighting a cigarette and taking a puff, Captain Tillson remarked that the quarters assigned to me had once been occupied by an early-day Adjutant's family, where a tragedy was averted by mere chance. The backyard was only a short distance from the deep, brushy gorge of East Fork Creek. One morning, many years before, the Adjutant's wife stepped out the back door with a dish pan. Just as she swung the pan to throw the water, an arrow shot by a hostile Apache lurking

Birds Eye View of Fort Apache, Arizona.
Looking East.

83667

*Corydon Eliphalet Cooley and his wife Molly in the yard of
their home, 1919.*

in the brush hit the metal dish pan and was deflected from piercing her body.

We walked out on the porch and, pointing with his riding crop to a high mesa a mile or so to the north of the post, the captain told me about Signal Corps Sergeant Will C. Barnes, who had received the Congressional Medal of Honor for his acts following the Cibicu Creek fight in the early eighties. The day after that disastrous engagement between hostile Apaches and the cavalry, Barnes got permission from the officer in charge of the few remaining troops at the fort to go to the top of the mesa and signal back any information of approaching Apaches or the hoped-for sight of the retreating cavalrymen. Then several days afterward, when the troopers had returned and the post was surrounded by the Indians, he volunteered to carry a dispatch requesting help to Fort Thomas, some ninety miles over the mountains and through hostile infested country, knowing that capture meant torture and death. As I scanned that mesa, little did I realize that some months hence at the same place I was to have an experience rounding up a group of sullen Apaches at a hidden tulapai drinking camp. To the south of the post my attention was directed to the high rimrock barrier and the general location of the only trail through the rocks, which the signal sergeant took when he left the fort on his dangerous journey to Fort Thomas.

Walking down the hallway, we stopped a moment on the back porch and viewed the adobe commissary, the guardhouse, and a number of other buildings along the back street, including the stables. As we approached the quartermaster office, I saw some Indian women and children leaving the post exchange and heading around the building. A few steps more and there, on a little knoll just outside the camp proper, was the most interesting line of habitations I had even seen — the row of wickiups, or tepees as we called them, of the Apache scouts. They were built with lodge poles and were similar in size and shape to the tepees of the Plains Indians, but were covered with thatched grass and pieces of old canvas rather than hide.

At the quartermaster office I was introduced to three white noncommissioned officers who were doing the paperwork. It was indicated that as soon as I became oriented to the post the acting quartermaster job would be mine, since Captain Tillson might be transferred on short notice to Fort Bliss, Texas. Again he spent some time signing reports and discussing supply matters. Then, hearing the troop returning, we went over to the stables. The horses were being tied to the picket line and some grooming was underway by the time the corral gate was swung open for us.

Before noon mess time we also visited the commissary, and there I met Sergeant Charles D. Hager, a white soldier who had been an employee of the Department of the Interior. I got to know Charley Hager intimately during my months at the fort, and we remained life-long friends. Sergeant Hager was sharp-eyed. A few days later, while the wagon train was unloading food in a back storage room, the sergeant caught two men of the work detail who had intentionally dropped a wooden case of vanilla extract and were draining the leaking box into a pail for an intoxicating drink. The soldiers were tried by me as the newly appointed summary court officer, and fined.

At the little eating place where we went for lunch, I met Doctor McLeod, the post medico. Since Captain Tillson had to work at the quartermaster office that afternoon, I went over to the headquarters for my horse, which an orderly had taken there. A spirited black animal was tied along the street when I stopped at the building with the doctor. A Negro trooper approached and, saluting, said my horse was ready and that the first sergeant had sent him over to be my striker and work for me, if satisfactory. As the doctor went on to the hospital, I turned to my horse, swung into the saddle, and started for the tepee row of the scouts.

There was some activity over there. I could see a few Apache women working outside and the children playing. But as I came closer the activity gradually ceased, and when I reached the area there was not a person in view. It was natural for these people to get out of sight when a stranger approached, and all had gone into their tepees. A closer view of the tepees showed them to be very interesting dwelling places. Long poles tied together at the top were used for the frame work, and the thatching was bear grass and brush, with an opening at the conical top for the smoke to drift out. Old canvas was also wrapped over the thatching for additional covering. On the east side was a kind of wooden storm-shed, with a board door for entrance. Nearby were additional ramada storage shelters built of upright poles, with flat roofs of brush and grass. The sides were open except for some wooden boxes stacked up for a type of wall. From the rafters hung a miscellaneous assortment of horse equipment, filled grain sacks, and ears of corn.

As I rode along viewing these primitive homes, an Apache scout came from behind. I spoke to him and he replied in very good English stating that he was Private Jesse Palmer. I asked him to come along as I had some questions about the scouts. He pointed out the post cemetery across the arroyo and said there were many graves there, from the old times, of soldiers and white people who had been killed during the Indian troubles. Emerging from the thickets along the arroyo I saw several Apache women with packs of firewood on their backs. One had a papoose in a cradle on top of her pack. At the scouts' corral were a number of ponies, and I recognized several which I had ridden the day before on the long trip to the fort. I questioned Jesse concerning the whereabouts of all of the scouts. Five, he said, were with Peasoup's wagon train; Grasshopper was taking care of the wagon camp at Show Low; and another scout, whose name was curiously spelled Tea Square, had left that morning for the wagon camp this side of the Cooley ranch. The others were on wood details making deliveries about the post; and Eskipbygojo, old Billy C F, and he were on the night guard around the buildings.

An Indian rode into the corral while we were talking, and he was motioned over by my escort. He was First Sergeant Eskehnadestah, but Jesse told me that everybody called him Chicken. He was about forty years old and a man of medium stature, which is the typical height of many Apaches. His face was rather thin with a long jaw, in contrast to the round full faces of his tribesmen; but it was a decidedly kind and calm face and gave him the appearance of a wholly trustworthy man — and such he was. His talk consisted of only a few words of English, but he was clearly a person of good intelligence and it was evident that more was understood than was expressed in that language.

When I mentioned that Captain Pink Armstrong was a good friend of mine, and that Pink had asked me to go hunting with "Chicken," there was an immediate change in expression. He grinned in acknowledgment and asked, "Where Pink?" I told him that Pink was with the 10th Cavalry at Nogales near Mexico, and he grunted indicating his acquaintance with the general location. Then he said, "You, me go Willow Kick (creek). Catchum deer."

The other scouts on the wagon details started to arrive, and I was introduced to them. Sergeant Chow Big and his brother, Corporal Nonotolth, were among the first. Chow Big was stockily built and muscular with the round, full face of the Indian. Both of the brothers were fine-looking soldiers, neat and clean in appearance, as were all of the scouts. On the front of their campaign hats were the emblems "U.S.S." for the words United States Scouts.[†] I noticed that Chow Big wore elastic arm bands, and subsequently learned that while on the Pershing expedition he had taken a pair off one of Villa's captured soldiers and wore them as a mark of an Indian coup.

My meeting with the scouts was somewhat formal due to their natural reserve, and I did not tarry long because I knew they would want to be alone to discuss the new officer. I thanked Jesse for showing me around, and we shook hands in parting. From the first it was my policy to treat the Apache scouts in a sincere and friendly manner, and such an attitude toward them evoked a fine response. Their good will toward me never changed even though at one time I had to confine several of them in the guard house for being drunk on tulapai, the favorite native brew of the area.

[†] Except that they had the additional "S," these emblems were similar to the type worn by officers as blouse collar ornaments. They were not "regulation," however, for the official hat ornament for Indian Scouts was two arrows crossed, three inches in length, with the letters "U.S.S." in the upper intersection.

III

THE APACHE SCOUTS

THAT EVENING Captain Tillson told me a great deal about the scouts, and I subsequently learned more. The enlistment of a force of Indians, not to exceed one thousand, was authorized by Congress in 1866 for use as scouts in the territories and the Indian country. They were to receive the same pay and allowances as cavalry soldiers. General Crook was among the first to enlist Indians, using them in campaigns in Idaho, Oregon, and Nevada before he was transferred to command the Department of Arizona in 1871. At Fort Apache that year he enlisted Coyotero and White Mountain Apaches in a company of scouts under the colorful Captain Guy V. Henry, 3rd Cavalry, and similar companies were formed at other Arizona posts. The scouts performed well in the winter campaign of 1872-1873 against the hostile Yavapais, and when General Crook returned to Arizona in 1882 to chase Geronimo's Chiricahua renegades he organized five new companies of scouts. Company A, composed of White Mountain Apaches, was stationed at Fort Apache under Lieutenant Charles B. Gatewood, 6th Cavalry; Company B, under Lieutenant Britton Davis, 3rd Cavalry, was first at the San Carlos Reservation and then moved to Turkey Creek a few miles south of Fort Apache. After the surrender and deportation of Geronimo's band in 1886, the companies of scouts were reduced in strength and eventually disbanded. Several graves of the old scouts were in the post cemetery. A small unit, denominated the Detachment of Indian Scouts and made up largely of White Mountain Apaches, was retained

[*19*]

in the regular service. They had a proud past, and I was now their commander.*

Captain Tillson mentioned also that the scouts had been sent into Mexico in 1916 to track Villa's bandits, but had small success because they were not moved to the front until General Pershing's cavalry was well into the country. They were, however, engaged in one fight — while acting with the advance guard of some troops of the 11th Cavalry — which aided in destroying the forces of a Villista general. Some months after hearing the story from Captain Tillson, I asked First Sergeant Chicken about the fight. Hesitating a moment to think of English words, he summed it up: "Damn good. Me catchum two. Sojer [soldiers] no [let] me killum. Why?" I later read a good account of the activities of the scouts on this expedition written by Captain James A. Shannon, 11th Cavalry, for the April, 1917, issue of the *Journal of the U. S. Cavalry Association.* It made particular mention of Chicken, Sergeant Chow Big, Corporal Nonotolth, and Privates John Cody and Y-2, who appeared on my payroll under his Indian name of Ka-Gethl.†

---

* A number of Apache scouts were awarded the Congressional Medal of Honor for exceptional bravery in the campaign of 1872-1873. *Decorations, United States Army, 1862-1926* (Washington, 1927) lists the following scouts as so honored: Sergeant Alchesay, Private Blanquet, Private Chiquito, Corporal Elsatsoosu, Sergeant Jim, Private Kelsay, Private Kasoha, Private Machol, Private Nanasaddi, and Private Nantaje. Sergeant Rowdy of Company A received the Medal of Honor for heroic action on March 7, 1890, against renegade Apaches while serving with the troops under the command of Lieutenant J. W. Watson, 10th Cavalry. The disbandment of the Detachment of Indian Scouts was ordered by the War Department in 1943. At that time the author was chief of the operations branch of Headquarters, Ninth Service Command, at Fort Douglas, Utah, and signed the directive letter dated November 30, 1943, to the commander at Fort Huachuca for the necessary post action. That procedure changed the Detachment into a local Fort Huachuca unit. This unit was inactivated on September 30, 1947, and all the scouts were retired.

† Two letters quoted in this article, which were written by whites for the Apaches, give an insight into the domestic life of the scouts. A scout's letter from Mexico to his wife, written by an officer, stated: "Some scouts got letter saying you crying all the time since I left home. Stop that crying. Don't let anybody borrow my wagon or steal my horse. Get some of your family to cut my corn and brand my calves. See that my children get plenty to eat. I be home pretty soon. That's all. Goodbye." A friend at the reservation sent a letter to

 · After the troop drill the next day, I went to the quartermaster office
to check the scout payroll. It was the practice to have all rolls prepared
ten days before the end of the month so that the proper denominations
of currency could be secured from the bank at Holbrook. Since the
January supplemental appropriation funds for the scouts' pay had not
been received from Fort Sam Houston, Texas, however, the roll was
held up for my review. The names of the Apache scouts, together with
some data from their service record entries and other sources, may be
of interest.

Name and Grade	Date of Birth entered in Service Record		Date of First Enlistments‡		Data
First Sergeant Eskehnadestah (Chicken)	Jan	1, 1875	Jul	3, 1893	Reservation number A-64.
Sergeant Chow Big	Jun	15, 1865	Jul	7, 1891	First enlistment in Co. I, 9th Infantry. Reservation number T-5.
Corporals Josh C F (initials only)		1857	Jun	20, 1895	
Nonotolth	Feb	13, 1872	Jan	15, 1905	
Privates Askeldelinny	Nov	1, 1864	Jun	2, 1879	Name was Major until 1898 enlistment.
Bones, Charles	May	10, 1878	Jul	2, 1891	First enlistment name was John Bones. First enlistment in Co. I, 9th Infantry.

one of the scouts saying: "Everything just the same here at Apache. Everybody
well. Your wife made some toodlepie [tulapai] and got arrested the other day.
B-25's two wives are fighting over the money he sends home. His wife B-17
spent too much money and his wife B-23 got mad about it. Y-2 [Ka-Gethl]
has a baby. It looks just like Y-2. Send me a silk shirt from Mexico. Good-bye."

Billy C F (initials only)	Dec 21, 1863	Dec 4, 1890	Early enlistments under name of Billy C J.
Billy, Jess	Jan 28, 1894	Nov 22, 1913	
Chissay	May 1880	Nov 3, 1913	
Cody, John	1871	Aug 30, 1900	
DeKlay	Jan 29, 1863	Jun 14, 1885	First enlistment name was Tich-Len. Second enlistment name was De-Chin.
Eskipbygojo	Jan 1, 1870	Jul 1, 1892	Reservation number D-15.
Grasshopper, Nos Chuky	1871	May 22, 1914	
Ka-Gethl (Y-2)	Feb 18, 1865	Feb 3, 1915	
Lane, Jim	May 15, 1887	May 22, 1914	
Palmer, Jesse	Sep 20, 1888	Jan 3, 1913	
Pope, George	Aug 28, 1875	Aug 12, 1911	
Pinintiney	May 12, 1861	Mar 3, 1893	
Quintero, Alejo	Jul 15, 1889	May 2, 1911	
Tea Square	1882	Jan 12, 1915	
Sye, Thomas	Jul 27, 1868	May 11, 1891	First enlistment in Co. I, 11th Infantry. Enlisted under name of Thomas Lye.
Tehnehjeheh	Aug 20, 1870	Mar 18, 1892	

‡ Prior to 1895 all Indian scouts were enlisted for periods of six months, rather than the Regular Army enlistment of three years. Hence the surprising total of thirteen enlistments for Askeldelinny (beginning in 1879), fifteen for Billy C F (beginning in 1890), and seventeen for DeKlay (beginning in 1885). Also carried on the record entries under each man's name was the comment, "Pay due for furnishing horse at 40¢ per day. Allotment for Second Liberty Loan."

It would be interesting to know the sources used by the recruiting officers and post clerks in establishing these birthdates. The Apaches had neither a written language nor knowledge of dates that could be correlated exactly with the calendar, and even the white settlers of those early days usually resorted to entries in the family Bible for such proof. There is every likelihood, then, that the birthdates of the Apache scouts were established by guesswork. The enlistment papers had blank spaces for such data, and according to Army regulations it had to be supplied. The dates of enlistment, of course, are not subject to question, and there is a possibility that Privates Askeldelinny and DeKlay were with General Crook's forces in the pursuit of Geronimo into the Sierra Madre Mountains south of the border in the summer and fall of 1885. The Apache wars were over when Chicken first enlisted in 1893, but during his early service he had been on several chases after renegade Indians. Much to my later chagrin at the lost opportunity, I never questioned Chicken about those affairs.

The oldest of the scouts, Corporal Josh, had once been involved in a tragedy, which I heard about in later years. White man's whiskey was at fault. In November of 1913 Josh had gone on a hunting trip in the mountains west of Fort Huachuca with Private Shorten Bread and his wife. The woman returned to the post and reported that Josh had shot and killed Shorten Bread. Josh was tried in civil court at Tombstone, then the seat of Cochise County, and acquitted. The jury perhaps concluded that the act was in self-defense. When informed that the jury had freed him, Josh said simply, "Wish Shorten Bread free, too."

The women of the scouts were well dressed and their children cleaner and better clothed than the reservation Indians. The particular style and pattern of the women's clothing was the same for all the Apaches. The skirts, made of calico in a wide flounce-like pattern reaching almost to the instep, showed the influence of the Spaniards who came into Mexico and southern Arizona centuries before, and was perhaps copied by the mountain Apaches from captured Mexican women secured on raids to the south. The waist was a loose affair with wide sleeves, and the body portion extended down over the top part of the skirt. Strings of store beads and sometimes large silver button ornaments completed the ensemble.

The footwear was the Apache buckskin moccasin extending above the calf of the leg with stiff soles ending in a wide turned-up toe, perhaps for foot protection in traveling over rocks. The daughters had clothing of the same design, but the boys were dressed in overalls and shirts purchased at the post exchange. A few of the scouts' wives and children wore store shoes, but they were the exception. The women styled their hair parted and down the back, but Chow Big's wife was different in that hers was cut across the forehead in a type of bang.

The family life of the Apaches was usually peaceful, well regulated, and happy. Most of their attention was centered on the children, who accompanied the parents wherever they went, whether on military duties outside the post, visiting relatives, long hunting trips in the mountains, or just across from tepee row to the post exchange. One day I went along the scout row and saw big, good natured Ka-Gethl, or Y-2, age fifty-three but a scout only since 1915, sitting on a box in the shade of the ramada. He was playing with his infant daughter, holding her by the hands and letting the little girl jump up and down in great glee. He saw me and grinned in pride. Stopping, I talked to him about his fine-looking baby. The wife came out of the tepee and stood around beaming with motherly pride at her offspring. Then I asked about the other children and a call brought them from behind the lodge. They took hold of their mother's skirt and peeked at me with big friendly eyes. It was a domestic scene of tranquility and mutual interest which was common around the camps of the average Apache family. Several hours later I chanced by the row and the scout was still sitting on the box, but now holding the little papoose in his arms. She was sound asleep.

Some time afterward I was riding up East Fork Creek looking for wild turkey. It was warm, and having hunted hard all day I drew up to a small pine-covered knoll and stretched out for a rest. From that secluded spot I noticed an object in the thick boughs of the evergreen. Moving to get a better view, I saw a cradle wrapped in a blanket and tied securely to the limb. It was the burial place of some little Apache papoose. Circling around and carefully searching for signs, I located pony tracks that showed where the buck and squaw had ridden to the place on a few occasions to look at the tree which held the body of their papoose. At least that was my interpretation of the tracks.

According to Doctor McLeod, the infant mortality rate among these primitive people was very high, and my observations were to the same effect. One day I asked Jesse Palmer, who had been educated at agency schools, if the scouts had married late in life since most of them were middle-aged men with small children. Even Chicken, who was well past forty, had a family of youngsters. Jesse told me they all married young, as was the custom, but many children had died in infancy. He thought that in recent years the government had been doing much to reduce the frequent deaths of the babies.

The habitations of the Indians and their methods of treating sickness undoubtedly made it most difficult to achieve a marked improvement. It was almost impossible to keep the tepees free of mice and rats because of the materials used in the construction and the Indian habit of throwing refuse around. The Apache lodges were miserable places in bad weather since they were not storm-proof like the hide and canvas shelters of prairie Indians. The Apaches knew little about health measures to be taken when a person was sick; all still lived in the same lodge and carried on their daily activities there. Those who survived to adulthood, however, were rugged individuals, and there were many elderly people among them.

Outside the post on a bench land above the White River lived two old squaws in a small tepee. They were so old that their bones seemed about to protrude through the skin, and one could move only by crawling. Commissary Sergeant Hager and his wife, Irene, used to take them food such as broken cans of beans, wrinkled and old potatoes, and torn sacks of flour, coffee, and all types of so-called "surveyed" commissary items that were dropped from government accountability. The post slaughter house was over in their vicinity, and the quartermaster soldiers always saw to it that meaty bones and odds and ends were given them. One day I saw the stronger of the two women collecting wood and to help her I used my horse to drag a fallen willow to their camp. The two ancient creatures grinned their thanks. I asked them if they were a hundred years old and one, nodding, said something like many, many years.

The old Apaches I saw at various places on the reservation all seemed to live away from the younger persons, but none were without food. Undoubtedly their relatives or neighbors took care of them. The monthly issue of rations at the agency never supplied their food, however, because it was eaten up in a few days by others who stayed around the old folks' camps on ration days.

A number of white people in authority at both the agency and the fort had at times tried to change the Apaches' habit of living in tepees, but with the usual disappointing results. Some years before, a post commander got the idea that all scouts should live in quarters since there were many vacant houses there. On a certain day they were all ordered to move to the assigned locations. An old quartermaster sergeant told me it was a sight to see the ponies with packs, squaws carrying papooses on their backs and arms full of things, dogs barking and running around in confusion, children carrying and dragging clothes, all heading for the quarters where the scouts were sitting on the front porches to mark the proper house. Within a few days tepees began to appear in the rear of the quarters and the families moved into them, using the houses for storage of their domestic possessions, grain, and horse equipment.

Sergeant Larzelere, who was in charge of the wagon train, had been at the post for many years, and as a young man had married an Apache woman. The family lived in a tepee outside the post, and used the sergeant's assigned quarters for a storeroom and as a place to keep his uniforms. They had a pretty little girl named June and two fine looking boys, Frank and Fred. These children were always clean and neatly dressed, and the best-disciplined youngsters a person would want to meet. Peasoup was a considerate husband and took good care of his family. Whenever he was in the post, his two boys followed him everywhere, and I know that he was a real hero to them.

A colored man in the quartermaster corps was married to an Apache who had a nasty temper. She always squatted around the quartermaster corral at times when he was laying over between trips of the wagon train, and constantly nagged him. He was a patient man and did not rebuke her. One day during one of her spells of belaying her spouse she became thoroughly aroused, and grabbing a pitchfork took after the fleeing Negro. Seeking refuge, he dodged around some wagons and climbed on a haystack; in exasperation the woman threw the fork at him. Then the soldier slid down the stack and walked out of the corral in the direction of their tepee, with his squaw following behind. I had seen the disturbance from a distance, but discreetly kept out of sight. At the corral one of the men told me that she was mad because her husband would not sleep on the ground in the tepee, but had moved in an army cot so that he could rest up while at the post.

IV

HUNTING WITH SERGEANT CHICKEN

As Pink Had Predicted, I had not been at the post many days before Captain Tillson suggested that I take a hunting trip with Chicken. It had come up one evening while I was visiting the Tillsons, and had asked about the skin of a mountain lion hanging on a wall. The captain had shot the lion on a trip with a rancher and a pack of hounds up in the rugged Mount Thomas country. Sergeant Chicken, he said, frequently hunted for deer and turkey over in the Willow Creek area, and usually brought home game. The captain suggested that I go out with Chicken on a hunt before it got too late in the season. Hunting conditions in the Black River country were still good even though it was already February and the weather was unsettled.

Preparations were made for a five-day hunt as it was a day's journey to the hunting grounds. Two colored men of the troop were secured to pack for us since it would take a couple of mules to carry the equipment and to bring out the game we expected to kill. Sergeant Chicken's eyes lit up when I asked him to go along. Grinning with anticipation, he replied, "Go any time. Speak when."

Next morning shortly after daylight I mounted my horse and headed for the quartermaster corral. Chicken was sitting in his saddle as I drew up, and, turning his pony without a word to me, he started in the direction of Seven Mile Canyon. The two packers had been instructed to leave later in the day, as we were going to hunt on the way to the camping place on Willow Creek. I followed behind Chicken on the trail up the canyon. Coming out on a plateau, we stopped to look around. The scout pointed to his right, and there was a band of wild horses under some trees watching us. In a moment they broke into a gallop with the stallion bringing up the rear, herding the mares ahead. He was a grand sight at that distance with arched neck and flowing mane and tail floating in the breeze. I looked at the silent Indian, and he was gazing intently at the fleeing herd. It was fascinating to be in the wilderness with an Apache. There was something about it that would appeal to any man, for the primitive is very close to the surface in all people.

Our direction now took us over a rolling country covered with piñon nut and other pine trees, patches of mesquite, and open meadows. Chicken centered most of his attention on the ground looking for signs, but frequently searched the thickets with his keen eyes as well as looked back as we passed along. Coming to a crossing in the trail, he pointed to signs in the dust. "Two Cher-cow pony," he commented. I looked at the signs and made out cow tracks and imprints of a horse. It was beyond my ken to figure out how he was able to decipher the marks and tell it was two horses. Especially baffling was his statement that the riders belonged to the Chiricahua Cattle Company, since Bill Ryan, Sharp, and John Earl, who was catching wild horses, all were in the country, as were some passing Indians.

We dismounted and got down on our hands and knees while Chicken gave me a lesson in the Indian science of interpreting tracks. He pointed to a horseshoe track that was over a part of another shoe track, explaining that cowboys' horses were usually shod only on the front feet. The overlapping tracks, then, indicated two horses, and the elongated iron shoes were the kind used by the Chiricahua outfit.

Going on a few miles, we entered a meadow and Chicken pulled his pony to a slow walk, watching the trail intently. Suddenly he stopped, and I dismounted quickly, yanked my rifle from the saddle scabbard, and came alongside. The scout pointed to a patch of tall grass several hundred yards off, and asked, "You wantum coyote?" Peering closely, I finally made out an animal head looking at us, and fired. The coyote jumped straight up and apparently fell into the grass. In an instant a coyote jumped up from the same spot and, as I shot again, went through the same gyrations. Then two others ran out, and as they crossed a bare spot Chicken and I kicked up dust around them. I was suspicious that my first shots had not hit. When I asked the scout, he merely commented, "Maybe so, maybe no." A search of the area confirmed the "no."

We were now traveling in the general area where years before some of Geronimo's followers and other Chiricahuas had been settled by the Army after one of their several surrenders. Chicken pointed out one place that had been farmed, but the brush had grown up leaving no trace of the cultivated land. I heard afterwards that Chicken's parents had also spent summers in that area along Corn Creek. His people belonged to the White Mountain Apaches living in the White River country and had few, if any, relations with the early-day marauding Chiricahua Apaches of the Gila River regions.

Big Bonita Creek had a deep channel but only a trickle of a stream of water. We watered our horses there. Some distance on the other side we came to a brush-fringed, swampy little lake. Chicken dismounted and, taking a single-barrelled shotgun from the saddle, started creeping up to the brushy shore. Close to the edge he stopped and listened; then, bringing the gun to his shoulder, he stepped out and fired as a flock of mallards rose and flew out of sight. When he came back, his only comment was, "No catchum." I noticed that saliva was running out of his mouth, and he was unaware of it. This peculiar thing brought to mind that Captain Pink Armstrong had told me the Apaches were as tense in approaching game as wild animals. He thought this might be a reason for their usually being poor shots, unless trained in military marksmanship. That also was my subsequent observation. I have seen other scouts sneaking up on deer and turkey with saliva running out of their mouths like hounds on a fresh trail, and shoot three or four times without hitting. Their great skill is in tracking, in knowing the possible course of the animal, and in sneaking up close, as well as in the exercise of great patience in lying in wait for hours at a game crossing.

Going on, we came to a timbered rough country and then into an open park with a small creek flowing through the far side. Chicken dismounted under a big oak, letting his pony walk on sideways to keep off the dragging reins for a drink at the creek. Here was our camping spot on Willow Creek. After the animals had been watered, I pulled my lunch out of the saddlebag and squatted in the shade near Chicken. I passed half of my food to the scout, he grinned his thanks, and we both ate heartily for it was long past noon.

In a short while he stood up, and knowing it was time for a hunt, I mounted. We rode through pine and brush-covered ledges and hills to the edge of a small canyon, where the scout stopped and waited for me to come up. He tied his pony and motioned for me to stay there, then silently disappeared into the brush. It was perhaps thirty minutes or so when a shot echoed from a distance up the canyon. Soon Chicken appeared and motioned for me to follow. We wound around rocks and gullies and part way down the brushy canyon for a mile or more before he pulled up and pointed to a gnarled oak. There hanging on a lower limb was a gray fox. It had been hit through the lower jaw, and I told him it was a good shot. Grinning, he asked, "Maybe you wantum?" Upon nodding my thanks, he added, "Woman she tan-um." I was pleased that he was offering it and that his wife would make a trophy for me. In a few minutes the fox was skinned and the fur tucked into my saddlebag.

Circling away from the little canyon, we found it quite a scramble to get out of the rough country. Chicken was some distance ahead when I saw that he had stopped and was peeking over a rim. Before I could catch up he had dismounted and disappeared into a patch of trees. By now I realized that hunting with an Apache was on the basis of every man for himself, and not on the hired-guide principle of pointing out game to be shot. When I got to the crest he was nowhere in sight. Then a shot came from down the brushy gorge near the bottom, dislodging a rock across the ravine. I glanced that way and saw a big buck leaping up the rocky ledges like a goat. Taking a quick shot I kicked dust above its back, but with careful aim the next one dropped the deer into a pile of rock. A moment later I heard Chicken shoot again.

We either had a lot of meat or just one deer. I walked back to the horses and sat down for a smoke. In a short while Chicken appeared, squatted down, and rolled a cigarette. I did not say anything, waiting for him to break the silence. After a couple of puffs he commented, "Me catchum one, two deer." "I catchum one big buck," was my rejoinder, and we both laughed — he, in part, at my pidgin-English, and I at our good hunter's luck.

We rode down into the gorge and cleaned two forked-horn bucks. Chicken was careful to put the livers and hearts in the flour sack which I had used for the lunch, and he cut off the heads and skinned out the bony parts of the legs. Then, leaving my horse tied up in the bottom, we started up the other side for my game. As his pony passed me I grabbed its tail and had a tow right to the buck. It was a fat four-pointer, and was so lodged on the steep slope that the cleaning job took a long time. I told Chicken to pack it on his pony and we would put his two young deer on my larger horse.

Leading the heavily laden horses, we had a hard time getting up into easier going, but finally made it between rests and stops for drinks of water out of our canteens. Just before dusk we came into the open park and saw reflections of a campfire and hobbled mules feeding in a meadow. Then the two Negro soldiers and their horses appeared under the big oak tree. It was a fine feeling to arrive after our long trip on foot, especially with a load of game. The two troopers came running toward us with shouts and laughter, and, taking our horses, headed for the creek to give them a drink before unloading.

Our camping equipment was under a canvas tarpaulin near the oak tree. While the cook prepared supper, I dragged out my bedding roll and picked a level spot. Chicken kicked up a bed of leaves, put down a small piece of canvas, and spread his Navajo saddle blanket on top. By the time the smiling cook sang out "Soupee! Soupee! Soupee! Without a single bean. Coffee! Coffee! Coffee! Without a bit of cream," we were all ready to eat. The custom in the army, and a proper one for all concerned, is for officers and enlisted men to eat separately. But this was a hunting camp, and to avoid any embarrassment I spoke up and said that everybody eats and the last man gets the leavings.

We heaped our mess kits high with steaming corned beef, fried eggs, canned sweet potatoes, and a handful of pickles. It was a contented group: a white man, an Apache Indian and two colored troopers squatting in front of a fire eating, canteen cups full of hot coffee setting on the ground, bread and jam where it could be easily reached, and the horses and mules standing nearby champing eagerly on the oats in the feed bags. Behind us in a tree hung the carcasses of the three deer, and off in the timber an owl was hooting. When we finished the evening mess and were stretched out around the fire, I asked Chicken if he knew where retired Sergeant Henry lived over on the Black River. He said it was maybe a three-hour ride down Willow Creek and south across the Poker Mountain trail in rough country. I wanted to visit the old timer, and with our luck of the first day the hunt was over.

Next morning it was very cold when we got up before daybreak. Eating breakfast and feeding the horses did not take long and after tying a hind leg of venison on my saddle, we were on our way for the Black River camp of the old cavalry sergeant. The two packers were still asleep under the tarp when Chicken and I left the camp. I had met Sergeant Henry at the fort on one of his infrequent trips there for his pension money and groceries. Ever since retiring from the 5th Cavalry years before, he had lived alone in the isolated canyon country working a gold claim and occasionally packing salt for the Chiricahua cattle outfit. All of his interests were centered in the mine even though no ore of value had been produced, but he had seemed eager for me to see it.

The Willow Creek trail was easy going, but swinging southeast across the Poker Mountain country was rough traveling. Several times I dismounted and led my horse, not wanting to trust his footing on narrow ledges. Chicken was cutting across and not trying to get on the roundabout and longer river trail. By mid-morning we were coming down a long ridge toward the bottom where we picked up a lower trail, and in a few minutes saw the sergeant's cabin.

The old man was out back chopping wood, but upon seeing us waved and shouted "Hello." As I rode up, he straightened his weather-beaten campaign hat, clicked his heels together, and gave me an old-time cavalry salute. Returning his courtesy and dismounting, I shook his hand for almost a full minute before he let go and likewise greeted

Chicken. The wholehearted welcome and overwhelming joy of the lonely old man sobered me for a moment. Then he ran to a pail on a bench at a corner of the cabin and brought us a dipper of cold spring water. Chicken untied the deer meat and took it around to a storage cave, with the old sergeant leading the way. Back they came, and then the old man rushed into the cabin and began banging the stove and stirring up the fire.

"Got a pot of beans cooking. How'd you like some and coffee?" he called, and then "Gad darn me! Forgot to tell you to come in." Inside it was neat and clean and everything in place like a barracks room. Over the table near a window hung a framed photograph of his old troop at a Saturday inspection on the Fort Apache parade ground. Then I noticed particularly that he was clean shaven and even his work clothes neatly patched and in good condition. The old saying that a soldier never forgets his training was exemplified here.

When we finished lunch, he dug out some old cigars. It was comical to watch Chicken smoking and handling his like a cigarette. Then the old man asked where we were camped and what luck hunting. When I told him that the scout had got two deer to my one, he chuckled and remarked that I was fortunate to have even a shot while hunting with an Apache. "Dang 'em," he exclaimed giving Chicken a friendly chuck on the back, "They act like a wild animal themselves, and shoot as long as anything's in sight."

Then he wanted us to see his mine. Following him around a big rock knob, we came to the tunnel. The scout squatted under an over-hanging tree, indicating he was not going into any hole in the ground; and we left him there. Inside we put carbide lamps on the front of our hats and wandered into a maze of tunnels, the old sergeant stopping at various places that were "making" gold. It was all a mystery to me, and I was glad when daylight appeared ahead at the entrance way.

Outside Chicken aroused himself from a nap and stood up. Then, pointing to a partially rusty coil of smooth wire hanging on a low limb of a tree, he asked, "Where gettum ticki-tic?" "Found it in a canyon over near the Bonita," replied the old soldier. Taking it down, he showed us the flattened ends of the long wire, which appeared to have been hammered apart with rocks. "Bet that's telegraph wire some Apaches cut out-a the old line south from the fort across at the Bonita to Fort Thomas. Could be, eh?" was his surmise.* "Anyway, when I first soldiered here in nineteen and o-five, a old signal corps soldier told me Geronimo's bunch cut a lot of wire the time they sneaked out of Turkey Creek for Mexico. Nobody knowed his Chiricahua Apaches was out on the warpath 'til clear past Fort Thomas 'cause the fort couldn't telegraph 'em." Biting off a chew of tobacco, he continued, "That wireman also said even during his time some crazy young bucks use-ta hammer the wire out-a pure cussedness. Maybe like us kids throwin' rocks at insulators and them street lamps. Ever do that, Lieutenant?" And I nodded assent, chuckling to myself at his realistic explanation for the youthful Indians' mischief.

After examining the piece of wire for a few minutes, we went around to the front of the cabin and sat down. As was usual when relaxing, the scout and I rolled a cigarette. I handed the tobacco sack toward the old soldier, but he refused and hustled into the cabin. In a moment he was back, unwrapping an elaborate meerschaum pipe from a soft buckskin cover. Holding it up fondly, he explained a crack on the curved stem. "A danged squirrel knocked it off the table and broke her clean off. But I got her mended good with glue last night."

He packed the bowl carefully with tobacco, held a match to it, and

---

* The military telegraph lines in Arizona were a continuation of the San Diego to Fort Yuma installation. During General Crook's first tour in Arizona (1871-1875), the territorial delegate, Richard C. McCormick, obtained an appropriation of some $57,000 for the construction. Under the supervision of General James J. Dana, chief quartermaster of the Department of Arizona, more than 700 miles of line were strung for less than $47,000. The construction work was under the charge of Major George F. Price, 5th Cavalry, and Lieutenant John F. Trout, 23rd Infantry. The line was extended from Yuma to Maricopa, where one branch went northward to Prescott and Whipple Barracks and the other to Tucson and thence northwestward to San Carlos and Fort Apache. When the author was at Fort Apache in 1918 the Army telegraph line extended from the post to Holbrook, where it was connected with the Santa Fe railway lines. A signal corps corporal was stationed there as an assistant to the civilian telegrapher. This line was used for urgent military messages, as well as for occasional messages to Holbrook merchants concerning matters of supply.

started to suck on the stem. His cheeks puffed out with the strain and the match burned clear to his fingers. Again he tried to light the pipe, and puffed and puffed in vain. A wild look came into his eyes as he examined the mended stem. Then throwing the meerschaum violently to the ground he jumped up and down on it, cursing loudly as the pipe was crushed to bits. I wanted to laugh at his tantrum and display of temper toward the pipe, and his acting as though the object of his wrath was personally to blame for the plugged stem. It was no time to laugh, however, because the man was so dead serious, and I controlled myself. Glancing at Chicken, I saw that he too was withholding his mirth, but had a twinkle in his eyes.

After it was all over, the old man meekly sat down, and with shaking hands rolled a cigarette from my proffered sack. "Gad dang me!" he muttered, "There goes my old friend of many years." Then, after a brief silence, he added, "Serves me right for my cursed temper." Trying to relieve the tense situation, I spoke of the activities at the fort and of Captain Pink Armstrong, who had been a recruit in the old sergeant's platoon years before. During a lull in the talk, Chicken looked up at the sun, and I knew it was time to be going as we had a long trip back to the Willow Creek camp. Bidding the old man good-bye and telling him to look us up on his next trip to the fort, we rode off. Neither one of us said a word for an hour or so. Finally Chicken pulled his pony to a stop, and pointing way back into the Black River country, commented, "Ol' man much jump." Then he laughed, pounding his saddle in imitation of smashing the pipe.

It was late when we got back to Willow Creek. The overcast sky and chill presaged a change in weather. After the evening meal I pitched my shelter tent halves, and told Chicken to put his covering in alongside my sleeping bag. The troopers made their beds down under the canvas of the pack equipment. By daylight it was raining steadily and almost snowing. Chicken stirred a little, and knowing he was awake I told him that we had better pack up and leave. He grunted agreement and crawled out into the downpour. We made some hot coffee, ate cold left-overs, and packed up. I instructed the troopers to stay with us on the route to the fort, and we pulled out in the miserable weather.

Left to right — Chicken, Jesse Palmer, Tea Square, Chow Big, and Josh C F, in front of the Adjutant's building.

Left to right — Billy Jess, Alejo Quintero, and Ka-Gethl, wife, and baby, at Scout tepee row.

Tepee row of the Apache Scouts at Fort Apache in 1918.

Apache camp on East Fork Creek. I got the ancient stone hatchet here.

As we approached Big Bonita Creek, I asked Chicken if the water would be up; and his "maybe so" meant to me that it would likely be a torrent. Soon I heard a roar of rushing water and knew there was a wild stream to ford. We pulled up at the creek and saw the channel was filled from bank to bank. There was not a chance of getting over the narrow space of fifty feet. Chicken went downstream and I rode the other way hoping to find a better ford or perhaps an uprooted tree that had fallen across. As I returned a stranger rode up and asked if we knew of a crossing. Soon two more arrived, followed by ten or a dozen hounds with some coupled in pairs. One of the men said they had been hunting a week for mountain lion, and were now headed for the fort to get supplies, not having eaten since the previous noon. I told them we had extra grub and would unpack on the other side.

In a few minutes Chicken got back and motioned for us to follow. About a half mile down creek there was a big tree toppled across a narrow channel, but the rising water was already splashing over the log at midstream. It looked rather treacherous, but one of the troopers took the end of a rope and crawled to the other side. Chicken got his pony ready for the first try, and we shoved the animal into the flood while the soldier, pulling on the rope with all his might, landed it safely. The other trooper started to crawl across to get the rope, and about midstream the hounds charged out on the log. I shouted a warning, and seeing the trouble he stretched out and grabbed around the log just as the lead dog landed on him. The splashing water and melee of animals made it look bad for a moment, but he hung on desperately as the whole pack ran over his body. Getting to the other side, he took an end of the rope and started to return. Then the excited hounds decided to follow, but he kicked them back as his partner ran up swinging a club and yelling.

Our horses followed in short order and then one of the loaded pack mules was shoved in. Chicken and I were now across, and both of us pulled on the rope because it looked like a struggle to ferry the large animal. It was half way over when I glanced up and saw that the other mule had broken loose and was following. Not daring to quit the rope, we pulled as hard as possible. Then, getting some slack, I tied my end to a tree and left the job to the scout. Running along the bank after the drifting mule, I finally got to a place where the animal shoved its head up trying to scramble out. With a lucky grab I caught hold of the halter shank, and my pull was just enough for a landing.

The other men, who had been standing around watching us, now started bringing over their horses, and with our help the job was soon done. We gave the hunters part of a deer and other extra grub, said good-bye, and were on our way. The route was now across good country. The soldiers came along slowly with the pack animals, and Chicken and I took a steady jog-trot for the fort.

V

THE POST MEDICO

DOCTOR ROBERT H. MCLEOD, a native of Texas who had been at Fort Apache since entering the medical corps of the U. S. Army with the rank of captain a few months earlier, was a congenial man in his middle forties.* We soon became good friends, and frequently I spent part of an evening loafing in his office at the hospital while he made the night check of such patients as might be there. Late one Saturday afternoon a Negro trooper was brought to the hospital on a stretcher. He was suffering from pains in his stomach, and upon examination Doctor McLeod thought it might be appendicitis. The medico ordered certain treatment for the night, and said he might have to operate early in the morning.

At Fort Apache the only help available in the operating room was a white medical sergeant. This man always gave me the impression that he thought his medical knowledge superior to that of any doctor. During a period when the post was without a doctor, he had extracted teeth. One of his dental jobs on the civilian maintenance man, Nick,

* Doctor McLeod doubtless joined the Army in the expectation of service in France. Born in Crockett, Texas, in 1874, he was graduated from the medical school of the University of Texas in 1898 and had practiced medicine at Palestine, Texas, since 1901. He had been a member of the Texas State Board of Medical Examiners and in later years he accompanied doctors from the Mayo Clinic on tours to Europe and South America. Between 1939 and 1947 he served several terms as mayor of Palestine. He retired from active practice in 1943, and died in 1957 at the age of eighty-two. This information on Doctor McLeod was furnished by his daughter, Mrs. Gordon Brelsford, of Tyler, Texas.

resulted in an instrument being shoved through the man's upper jaw bone and into his cheek. Such malpractice did not deter the sergeant in the least, however, and to hear him tell it Nick was to blame for moving his head! But Doctor McLeod was not one to complain. That evening he told me of some of his surgical feats. He marvelled at the self-confidence which he had developed without competent help and under the existing conditions. At the hospital in his home town there had been a trained nurse to give the anaesthetic, another to prepare and hand him the instruments, and a young intern or assistant to aid in the operation. Here the only help was a boastful sergeant who gave the chloroform and ether.

The following morning Doctor McLeod decided that an operation was necessary, and asked me if I wanted to observe. Putting on a gown, I stood near the operating table on the other side of the instrument stand and containers. The anaesthetic was started by the medical sergeant. After watching for a moment or so, Doctor McLeod turned to adjusting and arranging the instruments and setting everything in place. While doing this, he frequently asked the sergeant to check the breathing and instructed him not to give the ether too fast, to feel the pulse, and to call attention to anything doubtful. The replies to all queries were given in a cocksure manner to the effect that everything was proceeding properly.

Making a brief check of the patient, the doctor set to work preparing the body, then skillfully made a preliminary cut and the first long incision. The blood which appeared looked somewhat dark and thick even to me. Instantly the doctor looked up and asked, "Is the man breathing?"

"I think so," replied the sergeant hesitantly. Doctor McLeod reached forward to the head of the patient, yanked the cloth funnel off, and yelled at the sergeant, "Get the hell out of here! Damn you!"

Pulling the patient to the floor with my help, the doctor started artificial respiration by raising the body up and down. I grabbed where he had his hold and took over, and he worked expertly on the man's mouth and moved the arms. In a short time the breathing became normal, and we lifted the patient back to the operating table.

Wiping sweat out of his eyes, the doctor looked around and asked where the sergeant had gone. I found him peeking through the crack of an adjoining door, and ordered him to come back. By the time the floor and table were cleaned up, the patient was stirring some. After making a further check of his breathing, the doctor himself applied the anaesthetic. As soon as the patient was in proper condition, the can of ether was handed to the sergeant and Doctor McLeod continued the operation with speed and skill. All the while he was watching the application of ether out of the corner of his eye and giving instructions to the sergeant who stood with eyes downcast, pale and abashed, and giving more "Yes, Sir's" than I had heard in many a day.

As he started to sew the layers of tissue, the doctor looked at me for the first time and winked. Then, taking a deep breath, he continued to suture until the incision was closed, placed the bandages on the body, jerked off his gown and gloves and threw them on the floor, and walked out of the room. I went with him. Doctor McLeod was not given to profanity, but as we walked across the parade ground to our quarters he convinced me that a soft-spoken Texan might have a vocabulary adequate to any occasion.

The reputation of a good surgeon spreads quickly in an isolated region. The government doctor at the Whiteriver Agency frequently asked our medico to visit Apache patients whose cases indicated that operations might be necessary. Doctor McLeod made these trips by horseback, and I usually went along. On one such occasion we traveled for three or four hours up the East Fork Creek of the White River to an Indian camp where a long overdue and serious childbirth case had been reported.

As I tied up our horses, I saw a large group of Indians emerging from the tepee which the doctor had hurriedly entered. I wondered what was going on, but my chief interest was in the camp itself. I wandered around for some time looking at the abodes and the various items of equipment and trying to make friends with the shy children. In a couple of hours the doctor joined me and said that the family now had another young buck. Upon my remark that I had seen a number of Indians piling out of the tepee, he told me that he had to chase them out. But as he worked the doorway became crowded with young and old Apaches peeking in, and some heads were even poked through the grass-thatched sides. It was the natural curiosity of the Indians to want to watch the white medicine man.

An Apache boy now brought up our mounts, and we noticed that he was walking a little stiff-legged. Doctor McLeod, a kindly man, had become very interested in these primitive people, especially in the children. He asked the boy to pull up his overalls. Wooden splints with wrappings of calico cloth supported one leg. We learned that a month before a pony had fallen and snapped the bone, and the boy's grandfather had put the wood on it. A close examination was made, and the leg flexed and pressure applied; everything was fine. Upon leaving, the doctor told the boy to tell his grandfather that the old Indian was a great medicine man.

Soon after my first experience with Doctor McLeod in his operating room at Fort Apache, an apparent epidemic of appendicitis occurred among the colored troopers. Two more were operated upon within a week. Doctor McLeod told me confidentially that the last operation was not required, but he had been fooled by the actions of the trooper. There was no harm done, in any event. Several days afterward I was riding alongside Captain Tillson with the cavalry troop on the way to the drill ground. He noticed that the bugler was not in position and asked the first sergeant about the absence. He was told that the bugler had gone to the hospital with appendicitis the night before and was scheduled to be operated on this morning. The captain, who was wise to how such fads could spread among soldiers, ordered me to gallop to the hospital and stop the operation until he came to investigate.

I sped to the hospital and told Doctor McLeod of the captain's orders. The patient was on the table being prepared, but everything was stopped and the man wheeled back to the ward. Naturally the medico was irritated. "Captain Tillson makes me sore," he commented, "but maybe he is right. He usually is!" When we came in from drill later that day, I rode over to the hospital with the captain. In the ward the bugler was reclining on his bed, fully relaxed, smoking, and looking at a magazine. The instant he saw us, however, everything changed. Grabbing the ice pack from the floor, he began to writhe and groan. The captain looked at him steadily for a full minute, then curtly ordered the trooper to report to the stables at once for the grooming of the horses.

Even at military installations there are women who, probably for some weird idea of its prestige value, want personal visitations from a doctor. The post surgeon at Fort Apache had a few such "patients." One Sunday night long after taps a sergeant of the cavalry troop rushed to the medico's quarters and begged Doctor McLeod to hurry and see his wife, who was rolling on the floor in great pain and dying. Perhaps the doctor envisioned an operative case because he hustled off without his hat, but in half an hour he returned very mad. In reply to my sly question, he answered somewhat curtly that it was nothing but a plain old bellyache caused by eating too many pork chops.

A few days later Doctor McLeod received an emergency call from another sergeant of the cavalry troop. His wife was gravely ill, the soldier insisted, and would the doctor please hurry? I happened to be in the hospital office at the time, and noticed the deliberate preparations which the medico made. He asked me to go along, but I declined with a knowing grin. About an hour afterwards he walked into my quarters with a smug look on his face. "Well, Doc," I questioned, "how's the latest fad among the ladies?"

Chuckling, he told me that he had mixed a large dose of a strong laxative for this bellyache patient and had stayed there to administer the medicine personally. From his detailed account of the results, it was evident that the drastic cure would surely have an adverse effect on the social value of housecalls by the doctor.

Not all the post medico's duties were lightened by humor, however. One evening in early summer, Doctor McLeod and I were sitting on the porch of our quarters watching a brilliant sunset. A couple of Indian dogs, running across the parade ground toward some soldiers in front of the cavalry barracks caught our attention, and then we saw that someone was being carried on a stretcher to the hospital. Arriving there after a fast walk, we pushed through a group of excited soldiers in the doorway of the receiving ward. There on a bed lay a soldier with his eyes staring wide open, and his body rigid and still. Making a quick examination, the doctor asked if anyone had information about the sickness. A private said that the patient had been vomiting and saying that he was going blind. Doctor McLeod took action to empty the stomach. As I left, I saw another trooper being brought to the hospital on a stretcher. Before taps the doctor stopped by and said the first patient had died, but the second soldier was apparently resting comfortably. He was of the opinion that the men had been drinking something which caused the poisoning, and had informed Captain Tillson so that a barracks guard would watch for any further emergencies.

Army Regulations provide detailed instructions to be followed in case of death at a post. That night the captain sent a telegram to the deceased's next of kin, and the following morning was busy with many administrative details. A special order was issued appointing the doctor and me as a board to report on the circumstances and cause of the death. Nothing was obtained from our interview with the survivor except a belief that he was not telling the truth. During the afternoon I chanced to stop at the Post Exchange, and the Negro steward told me that both of the stricken soldiers had bought several bottles of green hair tonic the day before. That was a good clue; I located the doctor, and together we went to the barracks and made a thorough search. Under the mattress of one of the beds we found a couple of bottles of the hair tonic, one partially empty. Smelling the liquid, the doctor thought it was similar to the stomach content of the sick man at the hospital. When we confronted the sick trooper there, it did not take much rough talk to make him confess that both of them had drunk about six bottles of the hair tonic before becoming violently sick.

On the way to headquarters we happened to meet the first sergeant. He told us that Captain Tillson had received a telegram from the military authorities, and had ordered the first sergeant to make preparations for a full military funeral and burial in the post cemetery on the following day. Doctor McLeod wore a quizzical expression as he listened to this news. As we walked on, the medico said to me: "You tell the captain of our findings while I watch him blow up." Captain Tillson certainly did explode upon learning that the soldier had died as a result of drinking hair tonic. This soldier had disgraced the troop, Fort Apache, and the 10th Cavalry. The captain was going to stop the big funeral procession that the first sergeant had planned! In fact, he would not even attend the funeral! The captain told me that I would have to conduct a formal interment, but only so far as to comply with regulations and the customs of the service. He was going to request a general court-martial for the survivor. As soon as he had finished, we did our "Yes, Sir's," saluted, executed a military about-face, and left.

That night I secured a manual of chaplain's instructions and carefully prepared myself to conduct the interment. Right after reveille the next morning the captain came to my quarters and said that he had reconsidered, but only to the extent of riding with me in the army carriage to the cemetery. Over at headquarters after breakfast I saw the orders-of-the-day prescribing the funeral at 10:00 a.m., and knew that the first sergeant's plans had not been changed by the captain. As the hour approached, a two-seated buckboard drawn by a team of cavalry horses was brought to the captain's quarters, and I went over to join him. In front of the barracks across the parade ground the first sergeant was forming the procession, and as we started for the hospital at the lower end of the parade ground the procession also moved out.

A squad escort, armed with rifles, and the bugler walked in front. Next came the American flag and the Troop L guidon, carried by two corporals. A space was left for our buckboard ahead of a light wagon, draped with black cloth, which would carry the casket. Behind the hearse a trooper was leading the dead soldier's horse. On the animal was a black saddle blanket with the McClellan saddle turned backwards, and a pair of black boots tied in the stirrups. At the end of the procession came the mounted troop, followed by carriages with the women and other persons in the post who wanted to attend.

As we drove toward the hospital, the captain commented that he had never seen the black equipment before, but the troop supply sergeant likely had it packed away somewhere. Our vehicle drew into the halted column in front of the hospital, and upon signal the bugler sounded "Attention" as the pallbearers came through the front door bearing the casket. The route of march was along the road in front of the officers' quarters and out the east gate near the scouts' tepees, where the Apaches stood watching the procession. As we left the gate, most of the Indians joined for the half-mile trip to the cemetery.

The captain was silent as we rode along, but as we approached the cemetery he reached over and took the chaplain's manual out of my hand. "It probably would be best for the post commander to conduct the burial rites," was his explanation. At the cemetery everything proceeded with decorum, and as the last notes of taps died away the crowd quietly left the place. During the return ride the captain was without words until we neared his quarters. Then he commented dryly, "I spent a lot of work making a soldier out of that man, and look at the thanks I get."

VI

ACTING QUARTERMASTER

AFTER I HAD BEEN at Fort Apache a couple of months, Captain Tillson began to divest himself of the various military duties and titles and assign them to me. The captain's transfer to another station was anticipated at any moment, and he was becoming impatient waiting for it. Whenever the mail arrived, his orderly would go to the post office room and secure the military mail ahead of the general distribution. At the telegraph office the operator was instructed to be on the lookout and deliver any message immediately. Even Corporal Harte, the signal corps operator located at the Holbrook end of the Army telegraph line, was alerted to handle such a message as priority.

Captain Tillson talked over the possibility of giving me all the duties at once, but he concluded that it was better for me to be under his instructions for at least a few weeks rather than to be suddenly confronted with too many tasks. That course of action made common sense, and since I had finished college only the year before I was anxious to make a careful study of the Army regulations pertaining to paperwork.

Post orders were accordingly published making me the post exchange officer, post engineer and signal corps officer, acting quartermaster, and finance disbursing officer. These assignments were, of course, in addition to my regular duties as a troop officer and commander of the Indian scouts. Some of the duties were merely nominal, however, and all paperwork was prepared by the non-commissioned officers with a minimum of work by me.

[47]

I soon found that my most complicated and involved duties were those of quartermaster and disbursing officer. The only literature available on those subjects were the Army Regulations, which were as concisely written as statutes and without detailed instructions or examples. Sergeant Long in the quartermaster office had been a supply sergeant in a white cavalry regiment, and Corporal Cowart had the same experience. Commissary Sergeant Charles Hager knew nothing of the work before his enlistment, but was aware of government requirements from his prior job in the Indian service. These were all hard-working men, but they had to get their quartermaster knowledge on the job. Sometimes it was based on trial and error and sometimes on a guess about acceptable procedures.

Every afternoon after the regular troop drill, and often in the evenings, the captain and I worked together in the quartermaster office. His fundamental working principles included the personal counting of property inventory and the handling of all cash. These two things he emphasized over and over, and in all my subsequent government work I have never forgotten them. It was Captain Tillson's view that such personal attention to property and money would carry an accountable officer over many a rough spot even though his knowledge of the paperwork was limited.

Sergeant Long and I got started on a complete inventory of all government property at Fort Apache. Ordinarily a property count is a tedious and monotonous job, but such was not the case here. We dug into locked rooms that had not been opened since the captain took over, and checked obsolete items of early-day issue. The saying that only an act of Congress can dispose of government property was in evidence. We found old wagon axles, harnesses, kegs of handmade nails, pack saddles from General Crook's days, old-fashioned leather gloves with gauntlets almost to the elbows, a U. S. model 1899 carbine, old cavalry single-curb bits, a guidon of a troop of the 6th Cavalry, and even some infantry equipment. All of these things would be military museum items today.

Some of the inventory items then in use at the post had interesting military terminologies — aparejos pack, axles wagon hind, blinds pack mule, boats gravy, chimneys lamp, coffins, doubletrees, dredges salt and pepper, guidon Indian scout, hounds wagon, mills coffee, saws buck, wicks lamp, and buggies lumber. We discovered that, as usual in inventories, there was an overage of some property and a shortage of other things. The captain did not want to make a recount or a search, and so personally paid for the missing items.

Another job I had as quartermaster was supervising the wagon train which hauled supplies from the railroad at Holbrook to the fort. Insofar as I have been able to learn, this was the last Army mule-drawn wagon train hauling supplies to an isolated frontier post. Earlier all government property for Fort Apache had been hauled over ninety-six miles of desert and mountain roads by civilian freighters. This necessitated a great amount of paperwork and constant vigilance, but all supply problems were easily handled under this arrangement during the summer when the roads were in good condition. During bad weather, however, there was a constant shortage of supplies, for the freighters preferred to stay in the settlements rather than wear out their teams and equipment.

The problem of shortages could not be solved by stockpiling during the summer because the Department Quartermaster, located at Fort Sam Houston, Texas, would authorize requisitions only for current requirements. On one occasion the captain had tried to by-pass this red tape, and had ordered a winter's supply of blacksmith coal on one requisition, hoping that it might inadvertently be approved. Such was the case, but months later the oversight was discovered. I saw the communications that resulted. There were at least a dozen dispatches back and forth on the basic letter, including one from the Department Quartermaster General directing the Inspector General to investigate the matter. The final disposition was made by Colonel (retired Major General) Eli A. Helmick, who absolved the captain and recommended annual requisitions of coal for the fort thereafter. Helmick had visited the post at one time and therefore knew something of field conditions.

On another occasion Captain Tillson learned that there was a surplus of mules and escort wagons at Fort Bliss, Texas. That was in 1917. He put in a request for 104 mules and a number of wagons, which was approved. Sergeant Larzelere (Peasoup) took a detail of former mule-skinners there to escort the animals by freight train to Holbrook. In past years Peasoup had been a wagon master for trains operating in the Big Bend supplying posts along the Rio Grande. Knowing the temperament of mules, he wanted to match up teams while still at Fort Bliss; thus he would learn which mules were leaders and which were wheelers because, like soldiers, it was easier for them to work alongside old buddies. However, he had no chance to do this, for he was taken to a big pasture holding hundreds of animals and told to cut out what he wanted, then load them on the train immediately.

The railroad trip to Holbrook was without incident except for some slats on the cattle cars being kicked out. But at Holbrook the unloading, harnessing, and hitching of the mismated mules was livelier than a rodeo. Captain Tillson was there with a detail to help the drivers — men from Negro Troop L, the Apache scouts, and the quartermaster detail. At the rear of the L. B. Putney warehouse the supplies were loaded and lashed in the wagons for a clear run across the desert south toward Snowflake. Men on foot hung onto the bridles of the animals, some held gunnysacks over the mules' eyes, and others twisted the long ears to distract the animals until the hitching was done. Then as each driver started his two teams, everything was turned loose. Some teams moved out as tame as could be; others bucked and fought and got all mixed up. Two of the lead teams swung around to the rear, jack-knifing their wagons. Several mules reared up over the wagon tongues, their front legs landing on top of their mates.

Through all this confusion not a driver was thrown off his wagon nor a mule more than skinned up a little. Of course, a mule is about the only animal that can fall down, get tangled up and trampled on, and still come out of the mixup with barely a mark on its hide. The beast never loses its sense of self-preservation. About a mile out from Holbrook everything had settled down, and the wagon train was trudging along the desert road as if nothing had happened. In the rear, however, one wagon was loaded with lost hats, torn canvas wagon tops, drivers' lost bedding and the straw sacks they used for seat cushions, and other items; these had been gathered in the vicinity of the starting area.

Peasoup's wagon train was one of the best-handled outfits I have ever seen. His men respected him, and thus they worked with him without regard for hardship on those trips over long distances through heat, mud, and snow. One time just outside Show Low while carrying these mule-skinners' pay money, I met the wagon train. Rain had been falling off and on for a week, and the idea of bringing their pay was to boost the morale of these overworked men. Most of the wagons were bogged down to the hubs on a muddy flat. The others had made it across and were waiting, the drivers and teams helping to pull the stuck ones out. Sergeant Larzelere was on foot handling four teams by himself trying to get one wagon moving. He was plastered with mud from head to foot, and so were the animals. Up and down the line of mules he waded in mud knee-deep, a whip in his hand only to show authority, talking calmly to the hard-pulling teams and occasionally swatting one animal with his hand for encouragement. Once the wagon almost stopped, and he let out an enraged roar that brought the last ounce of pull from the mules. Then as the wagon moved out of the mire, he became calm once more and merely walked along, clucking quietly and spanking the animals with his bare hand to show satisfaction. When he got to the hard road, I came up and asked if the men wanted to stop work for awhile to get their pay. "Yes, Sir," he replied cheerfully. "They've been grumbling some about missing payday at the fort." And so their pay was distributed on the spot.

Always, weather conditions affected the work since twenty-eight wagons can cut up a dirt road even when it is dry. When it rained or snowed, portions would become belly-deep in mud. However, there could be little rest if the post was to be supplied. A one-day layover at the fort and the same at Holbrook was the only rest for both men and animals. It was natural that such continuous travel would begin to show in the condition of the animals, especially during the wet winter of 1917-1918. In March I sent the following letter requesting an increase in feed for the animals:

Office of Quartermaster
Fort Apache, Arizona
March 8, 1918

From: Acting Quartermaster
To: Dept. Quartermaster
Fort Sam Houston, Texas

Subject: Increase forage ration-wagon train.

1. It is desired that the following data be examined regarding the necessity to increase the forage for the 104 mules of the wagon train to that of Heavy Artillery animals.

2. Facts: weight 1000-1200; average daily trip on road is 9 hours; traveling 8 out of 10 days; average weight per wagon 3000 pounds; trips from Ft. Apache to Holbrook are 96 miles. November—3 round trips—576 miles; December—1 trip— 192 miles; January—2 trips—384 miles; February—2 trips— 384 miles. Now at Holbrook for a load.

3. The sergeant in charge states that the present ration is always cleaned up, and the mules act hungry for more.

4. At present the animals are in fair condition, but are thin.

Harold B. Wharfield
1st Lieut., 10th Cavalry, AQM

Someone at the Department Headquarters must have been a field soldier during his career because the increase in forage was authorized by telegram within a few weeks.

My duties as finance officer were made complicated by the paperwork involved. The payroll and the payments of personnel did not cause too much trouble because most of the troop clerks and sergeants concentrated on individual payroll remarks, but payments on contracts of purchase and property vouchers caused endless trouble and corrective work. Remarks from the auditor for the War Department, which I have retained in my files, well illustrate these difficulties:

May 1918
Voucher 35   suspended $45.00
Voucher 37   suspended $24.30
In each case proposals of contractors are not filed. Required.

Voucher 39   suspended $99.45
*Statement showing number of men present each
day & number of meals furnished is required.*
Voucher 41   suspended $13.20
*Voucher for hay paid Apache Indian A-48 signed
A-48. Full name and signature required.*

Since General Crook's time the fort had bought its wood and hay from the Indians. This practice kept them busy, and it made them independent by giving them money to buy things instead of begging for free monthly rations at the Indian agencies. The general also initiated — in 1873 — the practice of assigning a letter of the alphabet to each family clan and numbers to the individuals; during Indian difficulties a count could thus be taken easily to determine which Apaches were out on raids. This numbering system was still in use to some extent in 1918, and the Indians were proud of their designations.

Voucher 41 was for hay that A-48 and his squaw had cut with a hand sickle, packed to the fort on a pony and on the squaw's back, and had been paid $13.20. "A-48" had been typed on the payee line, and the signature was wavy ink lines of his "X," as witnessed by Tea Square, an Apache scout and relative. In order to satisfy the War Department auditor, I called in Tea Square and asked him the name of his relatives. The actual name of A-48 was a conglomeration of gutteral sounds unmatched by any phonetic group of letters I could devise. However, I recalled that A-48 was the Apache whom I had named Teddy Roosevelt for voucher purposes, believing that former President Roosevelt would not object to the hard-working old Apache being his namesake. I put that down, and everything was settled.

As established by Captain Tillson, payday at the fort was a formal military affair. This was done because this isolated place gave few occasions for a military parade in which the men would be interested. Early on payday morning a ride-around inspection on horseback was made of the buildings, the corrals, and the Apache Scout tepee row. At 10:00 a.m. all the detachments, together with the mounted Negro Troop L and the Indian Scouts, stood inspection on the parade ground, followed by a parade and review. Then in the afternoon at 1:30 the bugler sounded pay call.

The last formal parade and review at Fort Apache was held during my assignment as post commander; it occurred at a time when the wagon train had an extra day's layover for payday. Succeeding officers, up to the time of the abandonment of the post in 1922, considered the troops to be merely caretaking detachments. For me that last parade and review was a sight that has remained something special in my memory. I now consider it, in one sense, to be a final salute to the soldiers of all branches and to the Apache Scouts who were stationed there during the early-day Indian campaigns, as well as a farewell to the old frontier post.

On that day the mounted cavalry troop was assembled across the parade ground from the flag pole. Next in line were the Apache Scouts on their ponies. Then came the various detachments, who were seated in three mule-drawn ambulances, and on the flank was the wagon train. This unit had over a hundred mules hitched in teams, and in front was Sergeant Larzelere mounted on his favorite mouse-colored mule. At the signal for the parade, the troop started in column of fours before coming into a line of platoons in column. First Sergeant Chicken was at the head of the Apache Scouts, all riding in single file, and the other units followed in order. As the wagon train moved out, the rumbling of the wheels sounded like a regiment of horse artillery. Along the boardwalk in front of the Adjutant's building and the upper officers row, a crowd of women and children and other civilians had gathered, along with a number of reservation Apaches who had come to the post for a view of the spectacle. Each unit proudly passed the reviewing post at the flag pole, each soldier showing his spirit and bearing, the animals under full control, and the mule teams moving on the alert and stepping along eagerly. It was a thrilling sight for all of us, spectators as well as participants.

VII

APACHE SCOUTS ON A MANHUNT

My First Real Experience with the Apache Scouts in the field
was on a manhunt. The survivor of the hair tonic drinking spree was
tried by me as the summary court officer and given thirty days in the
guard house. Headquarters, 10th Cavalry, at Fort Huachuca had dis-
approved the captain's request that the man be given a general court-
martial, directing that appropriate action be taken at the post. Toward
the end of his sentence the soldier was placed on a trusty job during
the daytime to police up around the buildings. One day he sneaked in
the loading door of the commissary and stole some vanilla extract to
drink — with the results that he again had to be taken to the hospital.
To conserve manpower, it was ordered that members of the hospital
detachment be rotated as guards for the prisoner.

Before reveille one morning Doctor McLeod came rushing into my
quarters, stating excitedly that his sergeant had just reported that the
prisoner had disappeared along with two pistols from the office. Captain
Tillson was of the opinion that the soldier had decided to return to
Fort Huachuca, and thus undoubtedly was headed south toward Globe.
He instructed me to eat breakfast, then get a detail of Apache Scouts
to track the soldier. He emphasized that the man must be caught or
other soldiers might try the same thing.

As I stepped out of the mess room, my striker was holding my horse
on the road awaiting me. Over at the Adjutant's building I saw Chicken
squatting under a tree, and several Negro sergeants of the troop were

with him. Things seemed to be happening automatically, for nothing had been said beyond the captain's instructions to me. However, at a well-disciplined small post the underground messages from headquarters to competent sergeants produce efficient action without formal orders. I told the striker to go to my quarters for my saddle bags, which were always packed, and a pistol and box of ammunition. Over at headquarters I instructed Chicken to get five scouts and meet me at the White River crossing outside the post. Leaving word with the troop first sergeant to tell the captain that a scout would be sent in by evening for a pack mule, I rode towards the meeting place outside the west boundary of the post.

The scouts were ahead of me, sitting quietly on their ponies with government rifles in their saddle scabbards. Some had ammunition belts and others bandeliers over their shoulders. First Sergeant Chicken was off to one side awaiting my approach. Sergeant Chow Big had his favorite gray, and alongside was his brother, Corporal Nonotolth. Nearby was Grasshopper, and the scowl on his face reminded me to watch him closely, knowing that the escaped colored trooper had once tried to stick him with a pitchfork. On a jittery pony was Billy C F, a wiry little Apache well over fifty years old and a great favorite of mine. He lived alone in a makeshift tin shack near tepee row, and sometimes on an evening ride I would stop by for a smoke. As he was not able to speak even pidgin-English, our visits were just a quiet sitting together on the ground, looking at the late sky and smoking. Old Billy C F was one of the best trackers of all the scouts.

I told Chicken to instruct the men that we were just trying to capture the soldier. There would be no shooting unless we were fired upon. He motioned another scout, Jesse Palmer, to come over, and Jesse said that the trooper frequently hung around A-100's camp this side of the agency. It was evident the scouts had discussed the most likely place to pick up a trail, and besides that location would also cut across any track to the north in the Holbrook direction; therefore I immediately led off for the ford of the river.

We jogged along the upper road toward the Indian agency for a couple of miles, and were near a small farm when Chicken pointed to take a single wagon road toward some breaks in the mesa. About half a mile ahead was A-100's camp of several tepees. Jesse Palmer went over and talked to a couple of squaws who were working near a wagon chopping wood. After much conversation and pointing, he came back and said the soldier had ridden in there behind a drunken Indian after midnight, saying he was transferred and on his way to Fort Huachuca.

Chicken gave some instructions to the scouts in Apache, and they started their ponies at a gallop, scattering and riding around the camp. In a few minutes all headed toward old Billy C F, who was dismounted some distance behind a tepee. He had found a shoe print in the dirt. Their excited talk was in their native language, so I could only be a spectator. Old Billy C F and Grasshopper, leading their ponies, started off on foot following the tracks, while the others galloped away in the other direction, making a big circle toward the agency. In a few minutes all were out of sight, and I drew up on a ridge trying to locate them through my field glasses. After some looking around and wondering which way to go, I discovered them a mile away in the general direction of the drill ground toward the fort. I galloped over to join them, convinced that the best procedure for me was to stay near at least one scout in order to avoid losing them altogether.

They were following alongside a cow trail heading toward Kelly's Butte. Occasionally I could make out a shoe sign, so I knew the main track had been located. This trailing was easy for a mile or so — until the path came to rocky ground and disappeared. Here the scouts again spread out, several dismounting to look closely for a moved stone or disturbed clump of grass. It appeared that they were making good progress until they bunched up and pointed in several directions. Suddenly Billy CF headed south toward the White River. It was then Jesse told me that the tracks had been lost for some distance where a herd of Indian ponies had crossed the trail, and that they were going to circle the area to find out if the soldier had caught one to ride.

About this time Chicken spied Billy C F stopped on a hill. Evidently his position was a signal that he had the trail, for all the ponies were put into a run toward him. I surmised it was the track because the scouts fell in behind the little Apache as he went along at a trot toward the brush and timber of the White River bottom. I followed at the rear for a mile or two, seeing nothing that looked like a sign. When we neared the junction of Priebe Creek, the scouts all gathered at a sheltered spot made by the roots of a fallen tree. There Jesse told me the Negro soldier had been lying around but had left the place running. The trail led into a big patch of thick brush interspersed with bunches of high grass, which the scouts circled before coming back to me. Chicken rode up and said, "Catchum quick."

It was not likely that the soldier would shoot at us since nothing had been done to provoke him, so I moved my horse into an opening and shouted, "Private George Washington, stand up and come over here!" Nothing stirred, so I shouted again telling him my name. Still he did not appear. Riding back to the scouts, I told Chicken to have them leave their horses with Jesse, then we would surround the area and go through it. They all jumped to the ground armed with their rifles and moved off.

I followed Grasshopper closely, wanting to keep this grudge-bearing Apache under control and avoid a hasty shot. And he well knew why I kept so close. After a few steps through the thick brush, a limb he was passing swished back, hitting me full in the face. During the brief time required to wipe out my eyes, the crafty Indian disappeared. He had taken full advantage of my carelessness in being too close, and had intentionally bent the limb in order to slip away. An Apache on a stalk would never move a bush or make a sound. I was convinced that he had simply outwitted me. For half a minute I listened and peered around; then I heard a movement ahead toward the right. There the Negro soldier stood with Grasshopper's cocked rifle in his back. I told the prisoner to come over. He approached and shakily gave up two pistols without saying a word. I could see that he was scared speechless; who wouldn't be with this savage-faced Apache's rifle in his back, and it was kept there until I told him to put it down.

It was the middle of the afternoon when we started the return trip to the post. I had the prisoner catch hold of the tail of Nonotolth's animal to help him along, and Chicken led the way. Out of the timber we saw a herd of Indian ponies. One of them, a bundle of bones with a large saddle sore on its withers, was poking along the trail just ahead of us. Chow Big tossed a rope over its head; we mounted the trooper on him and were able to move faster, getting into the fort at sundown. This time Headquarters, 10th Cavalry, ordered the prisoner sent to Fort Huachuca for trial on charge of "absent without leave," commonly known by the soldiers as AWOL, and the theft of two pistols.

The problem of keeping soldiers contented at an isolated post and reducing AWOL to a minimum was well understood by the captain. Non-appropriated troop funds from the post exchange profits were spent for anything within reason that the soldiers suggested. Since the money was earned from a commercial business, the principle of using it for the benefit of all the soldiers was authorized. Complete sets of uniforms and the equipment for two baseball teams had been purchased, and a number of repeating shotguns for hunting quail and wild turkey were in the supply room. Over at the recreation building, alongside headquarters, was a player piano and all the current music rolls, as well as musical instruments and a victrola. A large library, with magazines of every type requested, were available. Writing materials, stamps, and tobacco were free at the recreation building. Billiard and pool tables also were there.

Whenever moving picture films could be secured, free movies were given with a couple of re-runs before returning the shipment. Well do I remember one show that opened in a bar room, the free lunch at one end, with a view of the swinging doors and sidewalk. Then we saw the feet and part of the legs of a man approaching. The shoes were oversized and the baggy pant legs wrinkled and frayed at the bottom. The person walked in a hesitant, funny manner, with heels close together and toes pointed outward. A road of laughter and loud applause came from the audience. The swinging doors parted, and in walked Charlie Chaplin. After the movie that night I carried the Tillson's youngest child home in my arms. He is now a West Point graduate, Brigadier General John C. F. Tillson, III. The captain was burdened with a sleeping daughter, and Helen Tillson, his wife, dragged along the disgruntled oldest daughter who had to walk.

The soldiers were well clothed and wore the so-called dress uniform throughout the day, using fatigues only when grooming the horses and on work details. Everyone had to be properly dressed for mess, and good decorum with a pleasant atmosphere was maintained there. The mess attendants and cooks all wore white jackets, and on Sundays table cloths were used. Much of the heavy quartermaster tableware had been replaced by purchased dishes. On special occasions cigars were passed out. Even a post garden was maintained and cultivated, and at times chickens and pigs were raised near the caretaker's shack where a hired Mexican gardener lived. It was by such methods, and a variety of good food, that the interests of the men were maintained in the mess; and never a complaint was heard. Strange as it may seem, a monotonous and badly managed mess has at times caused serious disciplinary troubles — and even mutiny — at isolated posts.

Despite such efforts by Captain Tillson, soldiers continued to run away. A couple of months after the capture of the escaped prisoner, a white quartermaster private secured a three weeks' furlough. He was an irresponsible individual, usually broke soon after payday because of his gambling in the hidden crap games held at secretive places around the post. A day or so after the white soldier left, Private Haines, a colored trooper who did odd jobs for me, propositioned me for a loan, giving as an excuse that the fellow on furlough had won all his money and more from other soldiers. Haines got a couple of dollars from me to clean and press my uniforms, which was an overpayment but not a loan.

At the end of the three weeks the soldier reported to Corporal Harte at the army telegraph office in Holbrook, and sent a telegram asking for a week's extension. In a moment of weakness I agreed, thinking it would only be fair to let the man enjoy himself away from the isolation of the post. However, that was the last time he ever reported to me. Some four or five weeks later a telegram was received from the deputy sheriff's office at Needles, California, to the effect that the man had been arrested as a deserter. After several communications, Wagon Company No. 4, Quartermaster Corps, at Fort Bliss, Texas, sent a guard to take the prisoner there for trial. The matter still was not closed because the deputy sheriff then wrote to me for the payment of the $50 reward for apprehension of a deserter. Government definitions and red tape are not always clear to a civilian, and the misconceptions cause much justifiable complaint. In this type of case the rulings of the Comptroller General defined the word deserter to mean a soldier convicted of the act; otherwise he is at most absent without leave, for which no reward is paid.

Much as I disliked informing the vigilant deputy sheriff that the money was not forthcoming, it was necessary. The following letter, after many revisions, was sent to him:

> Fort Apache, Arizona
> July 24, 1918

Mr. L. A. Bird
Deputy Sheriff
Needles, Calif.

Dear Sir:

Reference your letter this date would advise that reward under a Government ruling is not paid until conviction of the prisoner of desertion.

Your letter is being filed in this office and if the prisoner is convicted the reward will be paid to you.

It will take a number of months before this office will know the final disposition of the prisoner.

Thanks for your cooperation with the Government by having this man arrested.

> Yours very truly,
>
> Harold B. Wharfield
> 1st Lieut., 10th Cav., AQM

Months afterward, when I was stationed at Fort Huachuca, an officer from Fort Bliss told me that the quartermaster soldier had been convicted of AWOL. I never learned whether my successor at Fort Apache informed the deputy sheriff at Needles of the negative results pertaining to a reward.

VIII

ALONG EAST FORK CREEK

ON SUNDAYS I frequently left the post right after morning mess for a tour of the region, my favorite place being up East Fork Creek. An Indian trail went up this creek for ten miles or so to a fork where Rock Creek joined it. Several miles from the fort, in a bend of the creek, was a cluster of shacks in the timber; in these lived the third generation descendants of an early-day post laundryman, a Chinese who had married an Apache woman. The celestial's offspring had married Apaches, a Mexican, and a white man; the next generation had married to reservation people and to soldiers at the post. They formed an orderly, hard-working community. A few of the woman had domestic jobs at the post, a couple of the men worked for the Chiricahua Cattle Company during the round-up season, and the others were freighters at the Indian agency.

Beyond these shacks, the creek bottom ran through a fairly open country for a few miles. Close to the winding road were steep bluffs, broken occasionally by the numerous cattle trails coming from the high country down to the water. Near the top of a cliff, this side of Sharp's summer cattle camp, was a small cave in the masonry-like wall. I had tried to climb up to it several times, but was always stopped at the base. I thought the ruin was possibly a storeroom for the ancient natives and that slides had destroyed their path to it.

There were turkeys in the pine woods beyond Sharp's ranch, and one day I took Doctor McLeod along for a hunt. Fresh tracks and signs were everywhere, and the scratchings in the pine needles and grass looked promising. However, soon tiring of sneaking along quietly like an Apache, the medico began telling about a childbirth case at a share-cropper's cabin in Texas, which he and another medical student had officiated during their senior year. The story progressed to the point where the second infant had arrived, and his companion had rushed out to get the professor doctor; then a third baby was born. Bursting into a hearty laugh, he continued, "Then I got ready for more; and it looked like —" Before the sentence could be finished, a mighty whir of beating wings interrupted; then several more turkeys came running and almost flew into his face. It was such a surprise that neither of us could get into position for a shot.

Pointing out a little ridge upstream that commanded a fair view, the doctor said he would go to that place, while I circled the brushy feeding ground. In a couple of minutes another turkey jumped from behind a tree and ran off as fast as a race horse.At the report of my shotgun it crumpled into a cloud of feathers. Just as I picked up the gobbler from a fallen tree, another took a running start and flew off in the direction of the medico. A yell from me gave a warning, and then shortly followed four shots in quick succession. When I got across to the ridge my companion was seated on a log, his hat on the ground, his shotgun leaning against a tree. He was rubbing his shoulder vigorously. By way of explanation he said that just when I hollered the turkey appeared, soaring straight for him and landing right at his feet. His gun started going off, and the bird ran around the tree with him in pursuit. For some reason every time he worked the gun slide a shot followed, so he kept it pointed toward the fleeing turkey to avoid shooting himself. The doctor was a good story teller; and it was fun to sit there in the bright sunshine, smelling the pleasing odor of the mountain pines and listening to him expand on the incident. Finally we got up to leave, and in reply to my query about the unfinished childbirth story, he said, "That was all, but the professor complimented us on having triplets."

Along the East Fork bottom lands were many favorite camping spots for Indian families. Small tracts of two or three acres were located where corn could be raised during the summer months. The Indian

Service farm supervisor, Mr. Funk, told me that these tracts were allotted on a permanent basis. Some had such improvements as a fence around the fields, but in many cases the ranch cattle could stray in and out, feeding on the growing corn stalks. The Indians usually stayed around for a while, then wandered off to visit relatives or favorite camping grounds, returning only occasionally until harvest time. He said it was difficult to get them to leave the corn on the stalks to ripen, as they would begin eating it soon after the kernels appeared.

At some of the old camp sites there were burned spots the size of the ground areas of tepees. Charley Bones, one of the scouts at the quartermaster wagon shop, told me that those places were formerly homes where an adult had died. The body was buried elsewhere with a simple ceremony — or none at all — and then the possessions of the deceased and his tepee would be set afire. In later years only the blankets and clothing were destroyed, together with the abode. However, I have uncovered objects such as spoons, horse equipment parts, knife blades, and, once, a rifle barrel while scratching around in such places, never failing to find something. The Apaches have a fear of dead bodies and move from the immediate vicinity without delay.

It was customary among the reservation Indians living near the post to bury their deceased members in an area on a low brushy point near the troop drill ground. The burial spots were not marked, and the shallow graves were placed in small depressions, in mesquite thickets, on grassy ridges — just anywhere the survivors might choose. As far as I ever heard, the graves were never again visited by kinfolks.

One day the location of this burial ground was discovered in a somewhat untoward manner. I had the troop out for horse exercise in the vicinity of the burial area. The troopers were spread out in a long front moving at a trot, practicing handling their horses in rough brushy country and at the same time maintaining an alignment. In a patch of high grass one of the mounts fell, throwing the rider to the ground. The animal had stepped on the edge of a grave and broken through. Moving the troop out of there for a rest period, I rode back to look around. Scattered in the brush and high grass were a number of graves, all entirely neglected. The poles had decayed and fallen in on some; others had badger holes in the small mounds. There were a few bones showing through the caved-in coverings, as well as some scattered around by varmints. At all these places I put back the remains, covering them with dirt and stones to keep everything within the deserted graves. It was strange that the agency cemetery at Whiteriver was little used; but for some unknown reason the relatives preferred areas of their own choosing.

My quarters gradually took on the appearance of a museum. Fossils and rock specimens lined the book shelves. The gray fox skin, which Chicken's wife had tanned, was on the fireplace mantle. In a corner were several Apache water jugs made of woven grass and reeds and covered with piñon pitch. My ash tray was the top of an Indian skull, which some early-day army doctor had left at the hospital. Perhaps it was one brought into the fort by Apache scouts as proof that a renegade had been captured. There were stories about such happenings here and at the San Carlos agency near Globe. A large rug, purchased from a Navajo family visiting at Chicken's tepee, covered the floor. I especially prized that rug because it was brought across country on horseback and used by the Navajos for a bed. It is now, over forty years afterward, on the floor of my den, only slightly worn in a few places and the colors still bright.

A stone ax of the ancient peoples, who inhabited these mountains centuries before the appearance of the Apaches, was a particular treasure. One Sunday along East Fork I had stopped to take a picture of a squaw and five children sitting in the sun alongside a tepee. Over near a wagon a boy was tossing a rock around, and it looked like an instrument of some kind. He showed me the plaything, and it was an ancient stone ax. Fortunately I had a couple of nickels and dimes in my pocket, and we soon made a trade. Upon leaving I told the mother to bring the boy into the post exchange the next time they were at the post, and I would get him a candy bar for additional pay. When the debt was finally collected, she had all of the children with her; and they, including the squaw, left the PX eating chewy candy bars.

The rocky gorge of the East Fork, just some fifty feet back of the officers quarters, was a pocket of game animals. It was perhaps a mile or so in extent, covered with fir trees and brush. One day my striker, Private Carpenter, told me that a colored trooper had killed a raccoon there. Beaming at my interest, he added that the troop cook would bake one for me, "And, Suh, coon shure eats good." Right after drill I rode into the gorge, entering at its junction with White River near the west end of the post, and saw coon tracks. Farther up, back of my quarters, the trails were worn from constant travel. A couple of old coyote traps from the blacksmith shop were tied on my saddle, and these were set near the edge of the creek where the signs looked fresh. At my first chance next morning, I scrambled down the steep side of the gorge and got two fat young 'coons from the traps.

Sometime later over at the post office Mrs. Irene Hager told me that a wildcat had run out of their chicken coop early that morning and into the creek bottom. I told Ka-Gethl about it, and he said that his wife had a "Talkum hen, no settum egg" staked out under the ramada, and to take it down in the gorge for bait; the constant clucking would attract the cat. Following his advice late that afternoon, I took the fowl into the bottom and, tying a rope to a leg, tethered her to a bush within view of a rock pillar. The bait acted perfectly, clucking loudly as though feeding a batch of chicks and scratching leaves all around. My patience after waiting an hour or more on top of the pillar was nearing an end, and the sun had gone down. Then suddenly the hen started beating its wings trying to get away, and a sneaking form approached. Quietly moving the safety off my army pistol and aiming carefully, I squeezed the trigger. At the shot the wildcat was lifted into the air and vanished. The aim had been too low and only scattered the leaves and dirt under the varmit. When I told Ka-Gethl about it, he said to try it again in a few days; but I lacked the patience of an Apache to lie in wait for game hours on end, and once was enough for me.

Early one morning I awakened before sunrise and could not go back to sleep, so I decided to slip down into the gorge just for a look. Leaving by the back door, a few steps brought me to the edge where I peeked over. Near the bottom a gray fox sat on a rock looking up at me, and the sound of moving leaves was perhaps a 'coon digging for a bite to eat. This was the spot, or close to it, where years before a savage had sneaked up and shot an arrow at the Adjutant's wife.

The creek, as well as all streams on the reservation, was a trout fisherman's paradise. Every deep hole had a host of hungry fish just waiting to grab any kind of bait. Even a bare hook was sufficient if maneuvered carefully and yanked just as one touched it. During the spring months I frequently spent an hour or so catching a mess of the speckled beauties that averaged from ten to eleven inches in length.

On account of various taboos the Indians never ate the fish from the streams; however, canned salmon was a special luxury to them. Mr. Sharp, a rancher on the creek, told me that one reason for the taboo was because smallpox had speckled marks. The Indians believed the trout represented the sickness and therefore were not intended to be eaten. An Apache story held that anything living in water is connected with thunder, and accordingly should be avoided. Whatever the basis for the Apache taboo, it did not interfere with our pleasure, and fishing could always be depended upon to provide an edible meal.

A person did not even need fishing equipment to get the trout; at least, I discovered a primitive method by accident. One time returning from an unsuccessful turkey hunt, I got three or four with little work by punching a stick along a bank of a pool. It disturbed a couple of dozen or more, and one streaked into a shallow riffle and hid alongside a moss covered stone. A lucky throw hit close and it floated up stunned. This procedure was repeated with good success until finally the remainder disappeared. The trout were cooked in my mess kit, sprinkled with salt and pepper I kept in my saddlebags.

IX

OVERLAND TO GLOBE

SPRINGTIME ARRIVED in the White Mountain country in the early part of March. One morning I was made aware of the change in seasons while we were on the drill field. During a rest period I noticed a band of Indian ponies trailing out of an arroyo with wobbly legged colts in their midst. Almost at the same moment a trooper shouted as a jackrabbit fled from a clump of grass; then he called over some soldiers to look at a hidden nest of young rabbits. The captain had talked but little during that morning, and I wondered if the lack of information about his transfer might be bothering him. Finally he remarked that spring fever was a curse; it and the waiting for a transfer were making his life almost unbearable. Then, slapping a boot with his riding crop, he concluded, "Believe I'll take the troop to Globe. It will do the men good to go on a field trip. And there's a Negro community in the town which will entertain the troopers. Sergeant Peter's wife is from there."

When the order for the overland journey to Globe was read by the first sergeant at retreat formation that evening, some of the young soldiers let out shouts of glee that we could hear across the parade ground. Then there was a busy day spent preparing for the trip. Instructions had to be given to the medical corps captain about his duties, for he would be the post commander during our absence. His detachment furnished a mule-drawn ambulance, and the medical sergeant was placed in charge. Three pack mules were selected to travel with the troop and carry some of the kitchen equipment, rations for one meal, and the picket line for the horses. The blankets and bedding rolls, rations for ten days, oats and hay for the trip to Globe, and miscellaneous impedimenta were to be loaded into six escort wagons. There were three troopers in the guard house serving short sentences for minor offenses, but the captain decided to take them along for kitchen police so that they would not miss the trip.

The next morning, when the column pulled out of the post, the people left behind were on the sidewalks watching us leave. The dirt road for Globe was about a mile from the west boundary, across the shallow ford of the White River and beyond the drill ground. Here we dismounted and walked for ten minutes before a halt was ordered to adjust equipment. The escort wagons closed up on the troop at this rest place, and we rode back to inspect the collars of the mules and the harnesses. It was almost second nature for the captain constantly to inspect the soldiers and the equipment. Frequently he commented to me that the main justification for officers in the Army was their attention to the men so that the proper performance of duties would always be foremost in the soldiers' minds.

En route westward, Kelly's Butte loomed high to our left. This prominent landmark, according to some, was named for an early-day soldier who had sought safety on top when pursued by hostile Apaches. The first sergeant suggested that the fellow must have been killed there, for it usually took a killing to name a place. At the junction of the road with the one for the Cibecue country, we turned south and early in the afternoon clattered across the covered bridge over the White River. Our stopping place was not very far from where Grasshopper had poked his rifle into the back of the escaped prisoner. It was the first watering spot from the post, and the horses were ridden belly-deep into the stream for a much-needed drink. After lunch we went on across a prairie region to an overnight camping place at Black River.

Somewhere along this stretch was the place where the early-day post road out of Seven Mile Canyon, now abandoned, came westward for the Black River crossing. I watched carefully for the old traces, but so many Indian wagon tracks led off the modern road that the likely juncture was missed. It was along the Seven Mile Canyon road that many tragic endings had befallen travelers. Cattle herders, miners, and soldiers had perished at the hands of the savages along this lonely stretch of road. After the Cibecu fight of 1881 a civilian scout by the name of Owens, who was en route to Fort Thomas for aid, was killed there. Four Mormons returning to Utah from the Gila Valley died along the road fighting hostile Apaches. Yes, the old road from the post to the Black River ford had a bloody history during the early days as attested to by the headstones in the post cemetery, some of which were marked "Unknown — Killed by Apaches."

Coming down into the canyon of the Black River, the road was hung up on steep mountain sides for a distance, and then ran around a sharp point to a high wooden-plank bridge. Here we halted and dismounted for a look around. Off to one side were some dugaways of the old crossing at the river bank, and on ahead was the narrow bridge without a guard rail of any kind. The troopers were instructed to lead their mounts with a short hold near the bits, and the captain took the first platoon across in single file. Everything went along smoothly until about midstream the last mount broke a plank, but managed to get its foot out on the first quick jump. A soldier was sent back to mark the spot so that the others would miss the break. However, one of the animals in my platoon stepped on the broken plank but luckily lunged across safely.

This crossing was the only one on the Black River for all travelers coming from the south into the White Mountain country, as well as for those journeying back to the San Carlos and Globe regions. Ancient peoples, early-day Spanish explorers, Apaches, ranchers, and the Army had used the place. Before the county bridge had been built, the crossing could be made during moderate stages of the river over a submerged narrow rock ledge; but this was dangerous since the drop-off was deep.

Sergeant Henry, the old retired soldier of the 5th Cavalry who lived upstream some thirty miles, told me the story of an Irish civilian packer crossing there in General Crook's time. The man had an Army pack train, and one mule stepped off the ledge into deep water. The lieutenant in charge of the train shouted at the man to jump in and grab the mule. "Be damned if I do," replied the packer in disgust. "Holler fur one of your Mexicans. You got a lot of thim, but only one Irishman in yur outfit."

As is usual at such an isolated ford, many fights had taken place there when strangers and adversaries chanced to meet. It was the type of desolate and difficult crossing that was approached with caution in the early days, and not without danger even for the modern-day transients of the high, narrow, plank bridge. Even today many riders and cattle herds use the water crossing instead of going over the wooden structure. Before the bridge was built, the river was crossed during high water by swimming or on make-shift boats. The Army had maintained a ferry crew there at various times, as it was the Fort Apache — Fort Thomas route and had considerable traffic. But these details had been frequently routed by hostile Apaches. Once the entire group had been surprised and killed in the 1880's.

Our camp was established and the grooming of the horses was almost completed before the rumble of the wagons was heard up on the mountain grade. Previously the bugler had been sent back on foot to the other side with instructions that only one wagon should cross at a time. As the first vehicle came along and neared the broken plank the lead team of mules looked down, stepping over the hole gingerly with the wheelers following the same movement. "Don't have to worry about mules falling into such a place," commented the captain. Then he instructed the first sergeant, "When the wagons arrive, get some spikes from the horseshoer's stores and have a detail repair the bridge."

The next morning when we were about ready to mount-up, I heard a commotion among a group of horses and noticed that a trooper had carelessly tied his mount to an old fence post. The animal had gotten his feet into a strand of barbed wire and was rearing. Rushing over, I grabbed the bridle and tried to quiet the horse, keeping away from the wire that was being sawed back and forth in the hock of a front foot. In a few minutes the frantic animal settled a little, and reaching down I cautiously pulled the barbed strand out of the deep cut. As the wire was released, the animal lunged back and caught it on a shoe. The movement pulled the fence taut and a barb grazed my right hand, cutting the skin between the thumb and forefinger. It was a minor injury, but it left a permanent scar, visible even now as I write about the incident.

Finally getting underway, we started climbing up Bronco Canyon. Within a mile the rising sun blinded us at places near the top of the winding road. Some miles more across the high plateau region, a panoramic view of the entire south country stretched out ahead, with the distant mountain ranges fading into the hazy horizon. It was a sudden and spectacular sight. The troopers riding along at route-order, which permitted talking, suddenly became silent as each gazed in amazement at the far extent of the region. For some time along the road this morning the desert Gambel quail, with its blue topknot, had been seen, but here they appeared by the hundreds. During the balance of the day we were never out of sight of these pretty game birds. In all directions could be seen males and females with their broods of chicks scurrying out of our way and dodging around clumps of desert bushes. Only a few abandoned their broods by taking to flight, but in such instances quickly dived under nearby cover.

Early in the afternoon we came off a low ridge and down into a shallow bottom called Cassadore Springs. The early-day Apache chieftain, whose name was given to the springs, had located his band in a good area for water and living conditions among the shady scrub oaks and mesquite trees. Camp was quickly made and the horses inspected for sores on their backs or swellings on their withers. The animal injured at the Black River bivouac was coming along with the vehicles, the trooper enduring a jolting wagon seat instead of a comfortable saddle.

After the inspection I took my shaving kit and went up the creek to a convenient place. Hanging the small metal mirror on a limb, I dampened my shaving brush in the cold mountain water and rubbed on a cake of issue soap for lubricant in removing a two days' growth of whiskers. I had frequently seen Apache men sitting on the boardwalk outside the post exchange pulling out their scraggly beard with a pair of store tweezers. Each would feel his face to find a hair, pinch the instrument on it, and yank. Then he would rub the spot for an instant before starting to search for another whisker. My process of shaving with cold water and Army soap, even though with different tools, followed the Apache method of yanking and then rubbing the spot vigorously to reduce the pain. It was dark before the rumble of the escort wagons was heard. The first sergeant went over to the parking area to learn the cause of the delay. An axle had broken on the ambulance, and after trying in vain to repair it the vehicle had been left to be picked up on our return.

Before daylight the first call for reveille brought everybody out of bed into the chill of the high country. There were no stragglers for today we would reach a city — with all its changes from the isolated life at Fort Apache. The road meandered through fairly open country, and by noon the appearance of Indian farms were welcome signs of civilization. When we left the unimproved route and came up onto a graded highway, a murmur of anticipation was heard along the column of troopers. Now the wilderness definitely was behind us. Then I noticed a growing trail of black smoke rising from a side canyon, but for a few seconds I could not figure out the cause for it. Soon the smoke emerged out on a flat, and a locomotive with several box cars and a passenger coach appeared. Some of the young soldiers let out a shout of joy at the sight. They pointed at the train, laughing and talking in loud voices. It was the first train many had seen in months. For all of us it was a thrilling sight to watch the locomotive speeding along, the high wheels moving like an inverted churn, steam coming from the cylinders, black smoke trailing from the stack, and the cars bouncing over the rails. Then white smoke floated up from the front of the engineer's cab, followed in a second or so by the shriek of the whistle. The engine crew hung out the side of the train and passengers stuck their heads out the open windows, all waving at us. Every soldier returned the greeting, and even the captain swung his campaign hat in a circle.

Globe was not far away, and Captain Tillson sent me on ahead to make arrangements for the delivery of oats and hay to the camp grounds. We had left Fort Apache upon such short notice that the purchase of feed had not been negotiated. My instructions were to get the price from three firms, if possible, and order from the lowest bidder. In case the bids were the same, then to buy from the store nearest the camp and capable of making immediate delivery. My striker, Private Carpenter, came along and we set out at a brisk trot. Upon reaching the outskirts of the town it was interesting to see the shacks along the gullies and to look at the people. We rode down the main street with care, as it was partially paved with brick and our mounts were some-what hesitant on that type of footing. Private Carpenter saw a colored girl on the street and watched her. When she looked at him and smiled, I was sorely tempted to excuse him and let the boy talk to her for awhile.

The manager at the feed store where the forage was purchased proved most congenial. He took me into his office and pulled a bottle from a locked drawer. At that time I did not drink, so I excused myself by stating that while on duty a soldier could not drink and further-more that the captain was hard-boiled. I said that if the captain suspected that I had indulged, he would have no hesitation in disciplining me. The man was very considerate and asked me to stop by anytime to partake of the double-distilled moonshine.

I joined the troop as it was marching down the street en route to some vacant buildings at the other end of town. At the camping place a long wagon shed was used for the stables, and a warehouse made a good barracks. An office at one end had two large rooms; one became the officers' quarters and the other an orderly room for First Sergeant Key. The kitchen detail set up its facilities outdoors, using a large tarpaulin for the roof and sides. Across a small gully, steel carts from a copper ore smelter were dumping molten slag, and the sight caused much interest. That night this provided a particularly brilliant fire-works as the red hot material ran down the sides of the dump, sputter-ing and sending sparks and volcanic-like chunks bounding into the air.

As soon as the orderly room was cleaned, Captain Tillson started making plans for the troop during the two-day visit. In order to pro-vide spending money for the troopers, I was dispatched to go to town and get forty dollars in half dollar pieces. The captain had decided to loan fifty cents a day to each man who needed funds for entertainment. Before the end of the visit, both of us had fairly large amounts to be collected at the next payday. And, as was to be expected, some of the debts have long since been outlawed by the statute of limitations barring collection. All details for the troopers were made as light as possible, and only one guard post was established for the camp. The program provided for an hour of horse exercise in the mornings, followed by grooming, and then the men were free for the rest of the day. The extra stable work was taken care of by the stable sergeant and some of the mule teamsters.

First Sergeant Key was greatly concerned that the conduct of the men should reflect credit on Troop L and the 10th Cavalry. This was the first time the Negro soldiers had visited the mining town, and that was a special concern to him as well as to us. He called a meeting of all the non-commissioned officers outside the orderly room. We heard him laying down the "law" to them, stating that each one was personally responsible for the members of his platoon and squad, and that any trouble from a private would also be trouble for the non-com. The first sergeant was an old soldier and knew how to get results. Even though a penalty for misconduct by a private off duty could not be charged by military law to his leader, the men knew that the tough old sergeant would enforce his own penalties.

After the evening mess the captain and I went into town to call on an old friend of his by the name of Bill Ryan. He was at his drug store, where we were given a hearty welcome. Ryan had been in the cattle business for many years, and at that time his son operated a ranch for him on the reservation near Fort Apache. The best reason for an old cattleman owning a drug store was given by one of his cronies, who remarked, "Bill runs this place during these prohibition times so he can get a drink whenever he wants one." Plans were made at once by him to take us around Globe to meet the mayor and other officials, and to the Inspiration copper mine at the nearby town of Miami.

The next day was most pleasant, starting with a visit to the city hall and the county court house to meet the sheriff; then we went deep underground into the copper mine, and finally made a long trip to Roosevelt Dam. Stopping at camp late in the afternoon, we found the troopers busy preparing their clothing and toilets for a banquet and dance which the colored people of the community were giving in their honor. The first sergeant reported with pride that all the troopers had acted like gentlemen, and only one, who had missed the 1:00 a.m. check in, was being disciplined by serving as camp guard for the night.

The next day ended the visit to Globe, and shortly after noon mess the troop was marching down the street homeward bound. The boardwalks were crowded with people watching us leave the city, and many of the troopers' new friends waved to them, calling farewells. To me it seemed good to be going back to the Indian country. On the third day of travel, as we rode into the post, I felt contented to be at old Fort Apache again.

X

MORE MEN ARRIVE

UPON ENTERING THE POST the column of troops was turned over to the first sergeant, and Captain Tillson and I rode toward the Adjutant's building. At the captain's quarters Mrs. Tillson and the children were out on the boardwalk. Jumping off his mount for a greeting, the captain immediately asked for news of his transfer. A shake of his wife's head caused him to become stern-faced for a moment, but the happy shouts of the older children and the outstretched arms of his toddling son changed his expression. Extricating himself from the arms of the youngsters, he mounted, saying he would be back in a few minutes. We rode to the headquarters office where Doctor McLeod greeted us with the news that an army dentist had been ordered to the post, along with five medical enlisted men and a young cavalry officer, who was being transferred to Fort Apache from Fort Huachuca.

The doctor avoided saying anything about the lack of information regarding the captain's transfer, nor was he asked concerning it. The relationship between officers at an isolated station is so intimate that the problems of one, especially the commanding officer, become the burden of all. However, Captain Tillson was a good soldier, and he did not intentionally make his anxiety for the transfer a matter of our concern. Nevertheless, it could not be otherwise since we both admired the military qualities and the outstanding character of the captain. The quartermaster detachment was already at work preparing quarters for the dentist. Mrs. Tillson had an idea that the officer would be married, so Doctor McLeod, acting upon her wishes, selected an adequate house to be cleaned up. She was hoping for an officer's wife at the post, and had never ceased asking the doctor to bring out his wife and daughter from their home at Palestine, Texas.

It had been over a year since the last officer's family had been transferred away, and ever since Mrs. Tillson had been without a woman's companionship at the fort. Occasionally she had visited with Mrs. Peterson, the wife of the Indian superintendent at Whiteriver, but they had left the Indian service some months previously. The new Indian agent had unacceptable views to Captain Tillson concerning the use of the military force on the reservation, so it was natural that the strained relations of the husbands would preclude family social contacts. Mrs. Tillson had previously told me that on the first day the new superintendent arrived at the Whiteriver agency, he had requested Captain Tillson to furnish him a military escort for a tour of the Apache reservation. The troops were maintained at Fort Apache to garrison the post and for emergency purposes, not for reservation police duties among the now peaceful Apaches. The agency had its own Indian police and peace officers. The captain correctly surmised that the superintendent sought to enhance his own authority and to subjugate the military to agency control. The War Department's policy was accordingly outlined tersely to the new functionary, much to his annoyance and chagrin. That meeting ended all prospects for harmonious relationships; further dealings with him were strictly formal.

I recall one instance after my assignment as post commander when the Indian agent came to the headquarters office and lodged a complaint about the use of the reservation's dirt roads by the wagon train during bad weather. He refused to consider my statement that supplies had to be freighted in on a continuous basis at the fort. I immediately stood up at my desk as an indication that the interview was closed, and told him the proper channels of communications were by official letters through his Department of the Interior to the War Department. Disagreements and lack of cooperation between the military and civilian authorities on an Indian reservation were nothing new in the history of the West. It was the result of divided authority between the military and political appointees within the same area and over the same people. History books and the government's files are full of charges, counter-charges, and recriminations by both groups.

The new officer from Fort Huachuca was Second Lieutenant Marcus E. Jones, who had joined the regiment shortly before my transfer to Fort Apache. I had met him once at the cavalry squadron camp at Nogales, but even that short acquaintance was the beginning of our close friendship.* We were both enthusiastic about the cavalry. He had been raised in the horse country of Virginia, and was an accomplished and natural horseman. The cavalry was in his blood, for his father during the Civil War had been a hard-fighting Confederate cavalryman in Mosby's mounted forces. It was planned to have him share quarters with me, for the remaining houses were somewhat in disrepair due to a shortage of maintenance funds. The doctor busied himself making plans for the use of his additional medical corpsmen and preparing an office at the hospital for the dentist.

In a few days I was happy to greet Jones, who arrived on an evening mail stage from Holbrook. I was at the Adjutant's building when the vehicle drove up, and spied him on the front seat with the driver. He jumped out onto the rear porch as the stage stopped, and we shook hands heartily. The first thing he asked about was the horse herd. Was there a selection of spare horses for him? Had I already got him a good animal? Was the captain interested in horses? Could we drill

---

* Marcus Ellis Jones was born at North Garden, Virginia, on August 20, 1894, and attended grammar school in Washington, D. C. As a young lad he played at the White House with the boisterous boys of President Theodore Roosevelt. When he left the University of Virginia in 1917 upon his appointment as a second lieutenant, he was attached to the 2nd Cavalry at Fort Myer, Virginia. Shortly thereafter he was assigned to the 10th Cavalry at Fort Huachuca. Subsequent to his Arizona service, he was again at Fort Myer (1920-1924); then he was Military Advisor to the 389th Field Artillery of the Massachusetts National Guard at Boston (1924-1928), graduated from the Cavalry School Troop Officers' Course and the Advanced Equitation Course, and was at the Army Command and General Staff School. When he retired in 1953 as a colonel, he was Chief of the Texas Military District. Because of his service in the Philippine Islands (1934-1937, 1944-1948, and 1951-1952), the Philippine government decorated him on three separate occasions (see General Orders No. 142, April 4, 1952, of the Armed Forces of the Philippines).

everyday with the troops, or were there too many other duties? His enthusiasm was contagious, and I knew we both were going to enjoy soldiering together. Jones was a tall, blond-haired fellow, a fine-looking cavalryman whose walk was a vigorous military stride.

I laughingly told him to get all of his answers from the captain, but that my opinion was he would not be disappointed. Giving his bag to an orderly for delivery at our quarters, we went down the boardwalk toward the Tillson residence so Jones could report to and make a courtesy call on the commanding officer. Our visit extended late into the evening hours. The captain also was attracted by the new officer's enthusiasm, and especially enjoyed the talk concerning horses. Upon a query by Jones about trooper equitation and jumping the mounts over hurdles, Captain Tillson decided that instead of an intermittent schedule of those activities this would make a good half-hour program each day before the formal drill. I was most pleased to see the captain gain renewed spirit and interest in routine activities. Not a word was said about the captain's anticipated transfer. His entire attitude and talk concerning future plans seemed to be based on continued service at the fort.

Going back to our quarters, I asked my companion if he had heard anything at Fort Huachuca about the transfer. "Not a word," he replied. "As a matter of fact so little is known there about Troop L at Fort Apache that the adjutant had to look in the roster for the captain's name. He thought at first maybe you were in command." Such lack of information by our regimental headquarters should not be judged in the light of present-day administrative practices and modern communication facilities. Troop L was detached from the regiment and under the control of Headquarters, Southern Department, at Fort Sam Houston. Personnel reports were not made to the regiment, and only upon direction from the Southern Department were individuals of the troop reassigned or officers changed by a 10th Cavalry special order. Detached troops were always orphans in those times. We were by-passed in most cases when the regiment had openings for school details and other advantageous assignments of short tours of duty in other areas.

The next morning at the stables Jones was given his choice of several good government horses, which were always kept available for officers. He chose a small sorrel, asking if it would be permissible to change his mind after a try-out. The captain said he could have any horse in the group or make his choice from other spares. However, the policy of exempting the troopers' assigned mounts was explained. The reasons given were based on maintaining the soldiers' morale and pride in their own horses. Furthermore, the captain thought the policy was proper because military law provided forage and care for a certain number of mounts owned by officers, which indicated the desirability of keeping the government animals for the troopers. He did not think this intent was weakened even though officers below field grade were not specifically required to provide a personal mount.

Prior to coming to Fort Apache I saw this common-sense cavalry custom preserved in a most diplomatic manner by First Sergeant Thomas Jordon of Troop F. A "ninety day wonder," the term used by soldiers for recent graduates of the officers' training schools, was assigned as commanding officer of that company. He picked out a horse which a corporal had trained for several years, and told the first sergeant that would be his choice. First Sergeant Jordon solemnly blinked his eyes in bewilderment. Then a thought came to his mind. "Captain," he said, "Dat hoss never let nobody 'cept the corporal ride him. Maybe you want one of dem good extra ones 'til you buy a personal mount like all you regular Army officers." Perhaps it was a snap judgment on the sergeant's part that the newly commissioned captain would want to be treated the same as a regular cavalry officer. But knowing the wisdom and keen perception of human nature, which was a well-known characteristic of the old sergeant, we junior officers believed it was decidedly a diplomatic move. Anyway, the captain decided on a mount from the unassigned group.

The following evening the dental officer arrived, and true to Mrs. Tillson's intuition a lady was with him. The young dentist and his bride of a few months added much to our activities; the young woman was especially welcome, for she afforded the captain's wife a chance for the female companionship she craved. So much did she yearn for the association of another woman that she almost haunted the quarters of the young wife for a couple of weeks. One time I heard the captain gently calling the matter to her attention. We officers at the post, other than the captain, naturally had no conception or knowledge of the void in Mrs. Tillson's life in that respect. We were too busy and too interested with our own affairs to pay any attention to a married woman's concerns.

Years later Esther Buchanan Smith, who was the assistant postmistress at Fort Huachuca during my service with the regiment, told me of another incident of an Army wife's loneliness. Although the case was very different from our circumstances at Fort Apache, the plight of the woman reminded me of Mrs. Tillson's case. The incident was brought about by general court-martial charges against a West Point officer, who had a fist-fight on the parade ground with a junior officer. His somewhat reserved young wife, perhaps feeling she was defending her husband, isolated herself from the post people with whom they had social relations. Their intimate contacts had naturally been within the circle of regular Army people.

In those times the regulars were a most potent force at the military establishments. Their customs were a rigid code developed throughout the years of life at farflung posts. It was in some sense a common-law growth of customs best suited to promote harmonious relations between the officers and families in the close-knit community life, and to maintain a high standard of officer conduct and aims. Should any officer become the subject for a military trial involving his personal integrity, he was left unto himself until the formal verdict. Each officer was solely responsible for his own career, and knew that he alone had to solve his troubles. In this type of case it was considered necessary for the accused officer to quarantine himself socially until such time as he might be exonerated. By such action all were relieved of possible embarrassment.

One evening as Esther was passing that officer's quarters, returning to the post office for some work, the wife called to her and asked if she could walk along and get some stamps. It was most surprising since the woman had never before so much as deigned to speak to the postmistress. The young wife appeared dejected, but tried hard to be agreeable; then suddenly she burst into sobs. She told Esther that the loneliness and the isolation from her friends was unbearable, making her despondent, and she wondered if it were all worthwhile. All she wanted was to walk along with the postmistress, saying she hoped her presence would not jeopardize Esther's job at the post office. The young wife sat on the porch of the building until closing time, then, apparently under control, returned to her home.

Lieutenant Jones was assigned the position of Post Exchange officer, and also made Adjutant. In my files is one of the first items of his administrative work.

Fort Apache, Arizona'
April 8, 1918

Detail for to-morrow:

For Officer of the Day:

    1st Lieut. Harold B. Wharfield

      By order of Captain Tillson, Jr.

Marcus E. Jones
2d Lieut., 10th Cavalry
Adjutant.

Several days previously we had taken a ride toward the Whiteriver agency and across to the East Fork so I could show Jones some of the Indian camps and patches of farms. On our return trip we saw several Apaches galloping across country toward a group of tepees located near a corn field. Riding past the abodes, we spied several men stumbling around and leering at us. They appeared drunk. The matter was outside our jurisdiction, so we continued on without an investigation. Upon returning to the post, I reported the affair to the captain, and he in turn sent word to the authorities at the agency. He told us it was the time of year when the kernels of corn were just the right size for making tulapai, and the drinking bouts were the curse of a number of the Apaches. However, the majority of the Indians avoided the troubles of the riotous few by abstinence. The old Apache custom that intoxicating drink was the special indulgence reserved for the chiefs and principal warriors still had its followers.

Tulapai, sometimes called tizwin, is an alcoholic drink made from young corn. The kernels are put to soak in water, and the mixture heated slowly for a number of hours until the corn and fluid becomes a mash. Then the tin tub, or big can container, is put in a shady spot to ferment. Within a few days the sampling and testing of the souring beverage by the adult members of the group develops into a serious drinking bout. At no time have I ever heard of the children being involved; they play by themselves and keep out of the way of the grown-ups. It takes huge quantities of the sour-smelling, vile concoction to produce intoxication; but an Indian has plenty of time and sits drinking by the hour. The accompanying revolt of the physical system against such abuse is usually evidenced by frequent retching and vomiting. Such temporary discomfort is no deterrent to the individuals, however. It merely causes a brief pause in their festivities.

The news that a tulapai party had started traveled fast, and the drinking friends would begin gathering at the camps. I soon learned that the sight of two or three bucks in a group galloping across country was a sure sign that a drinking party was in progress somewhere. The squaws went to the celebration at a slower gait, being encumbered with papooses on their backs and their flocks of children. However, they usually arrived in time to get their share of the liquor. The chief danger in this type of indulgence among these people was due to the nature of the Apache. When intoxicated, they recall all past grudges and petty differences, and easily lose their sense of self-control and judgment. Shortly before my arrival at the post, one of the Apache scouts and a reservation Indian had a rifle fight while intoxicated. They deliberately posted themselves on opposite sides of a narrow gorge in Seven Mile Canyon, and then started shooting at each other. It was a type of formal duel, not the usual rough and ready methods used by most of the drunks who perpetrated their revenge without warning.

The next day after Jones and I passed through the agency, while walking toward headquarters, I noticed a guard taking a squaw into the building. She was the wife of the Apache scout who previously had

Chow Big and Wharfield have their picture taken together.

Troop L stacks arms at the rifle range.

The drum and bugle corps helped the "monkey drill" go through its routines.

Troops riding Roman style at Fort Apache.

fought the duel in Seven Mile Canyon. As they passed me, the sour smell of tulapai permeated the air and she hung back from the soldier, who had a firm grip on her arm. At that time she had the family tepee located outside the post proper in the direction of the water reservoir. A scout had told me she was quite quarrelsome with her neighbors on scout row; therefore her husband had made her move in order to have domestic peace around the home. Indians enjoy gossip about their neighbors, and the men by far outdo any white woman. I usually let the scouts gossip to me without any comments, knowing it was their custom, and, also, they were considering me as one of them.

When Captain Tillson arrived at the Adjutant's building, the woman was taken into his office. I could hear him talking quite severely to her; then she came out crestfallen and scared. The captain told me that he had first sighted her going through the post area toward the scout row carrying a five-gallon can. When the squaw saw him riding in that section, she dodged into a stable; but he easily traced her by the smell of tulapai to a pile of hay. A leg was sticking out, so the culprit was located without any prodding. In the office he had threatened to have her removed from the vicinity of the post if she were again caught with tulapai. She was a pretty good mother to her brood of children and had plenty of domestic problems with her spouse, so the captain hoped the scare might be sufficient in her case. He had sent for the Indian scout, knowing that the husband was a partner in the liquor matter, and he intended to give the Apache an old-fashioned Army "skinning."

It was decided that we three troop officers would take turns making a midnight inspection of the guard and a tour of the buildings for a couple of weeks. Several of the scouts were particular objects of concern during the tulapai season. I took the first assignment of duty as Officer of the Day, and got up shortly after midnight for an inspection. Over at the stables I did not bother to saddle-up, mounting bareback and using the halter shank to guide my horse. The trooper at the guard house reported everything in order, and that he had seen Pinintiney only a few minutes before riding the scout post around the fort. After making the circle of the buildings, I returned my horse to the stable, then walked over to scout row for a final inspection.

A big full moon was getting low in the sky, and the myriad stars appeared like a canopy over the post and surrounding ridges of the rimrock. Everything was quiet and peaceful. As I passed around one end of tepee row, something touched the seat of my riding breeches sending me up into the air in an instinctive leap. An Indian dog slouched away with his tail drawn tight between his legs. Most of the mongrels there were friendly because on my frequent visits I usually brought along a handful of kitchen scraps or soda crackers from the post exchange as a bribe. One of them, Pancho I had named him, had come up behind me making a friendly gesture, and both of us had been scared off. Squatting down, I tried to get the dog to come back and be petted, but he kept a safe distance and wagged his tail.

Continuing on, I heard sounds like muffled singing. Near the end of the row a small light showed from a tepee, and the primitive music came from there. Moving along quietly, I approached the doorway and bent low to peer inside. A group of scouts and their women were sitting around a little fire, singing low in guttural tones. They stopped and one, taking a pot from the edge of the fire, filled a big tin cup and passed it around. I could smell the odor of coffee, so I knew that it was no tulapai party. A small bundle of blankets near the outer edge of the circle moved, and a deep throated cough came from the folds. Reaching over, a woman moved the bundle back and forth in a rocking movement. Then a weak cry came forth, followed by a series of coughs. All eyes were turned toward the mother, who continued rocking the covered form. I was witnessing a scene of Apache life that was founded deep in the lore of their savage existence. They were engaged in singing a healing chant of their tribe. It was an ancient ceremony in which they placed their full faith of a cure for the sick child.

I recalled that Dr. McLeod had told me one of Jesse Palmer's children had a touch of pneumonia, and the parents had resisted all suggestions about moving the youngster to the hospital. Jesse was the best-educated Apache scout; he had attended an Indian school in southern Arizona for some time, and talked like a white man. During all of my conversations and contacts it never entered my mind that he was anything but one of us in all things. Evidently, however, his

Apache customs were still strong insofar as curing his own child was concerned. When the little one became quiet, the guttural chant was resumed. I could see dour-faced Grasshopper squatted in the circle, muttering the song. There, too, was Chicken rocking back and forth as he sang. Nonotolth was seated next to his brother, Chow Big. My friend old Billy C F was there looking intently into the glow of the little fire. Several Apache women, whom I could not identify, were seated in the circle, and the remainder were squatting in the shadows back of the group. The other children of the family were likely the forms wrapped in blankets near the further edge of the tepee. One old squaw had a single blanket around her body and was curled up near the fire. Jesse was raised up on a knee, and I thought he appeared occupied with activities as host of the ceremony in his abode.

After a few minutes my legs became cramped, and I quietly withdrew to a place near a brush ramada. Low in the sky, the full moon was now nearing the distant bare peak of Old Baldy, and casting an eerie light over scout row. Pancho sneaked up and squatted at my feet. The low guttural chant of the Apache healing song continued in the nearby tepee. It was a fascinating and strange experience, one few white men witness.

XI

EXPLORING FOR INDIAN RUINS

MY STRIKER EXCITED MY CURIOSITY on one occasion by telling me about a cave up East Fork Creek that was between Sharp's Ranch and the storage room high on the cliffs I had previously tried to reach. I had never seen this cave on my trips to the vicinity, so I suggested to Lieutenant Jones that on the next Saturday we go exploring, taking along our strikers to point out the exact location. Plans were made to have the two soldiers drive a buckboard to the place with picks, shovels, and all the likely equipment that might be necessary. I secured a ball of heavy string, as well as some candles to use as supplements for flashlights. We were then ready to do some cave exploring.

When Saturday arrived, our group set out immediately after the morning inspection. Jones and I left ahead of the troopers for the agreed-upon rendezvous. Several miles from the post, while passing a corn field, Jones urged his mount to a canter and took a shot with his .45 pistol at a piece of cloth tied to a stick, a crude scarecrow devised by an Indian farmer. The sound frightened three or four ravens from the center of the field, and we both took snap shots at the flying birds. A cloud of feathers erupted from one, and it came tumbling to the ground; this was such a surprise and a piece of sheer luck that neither of us would claim the shot, but we did shout and laugh about it. Our hilarity was cut short, however, by a squaw who emerged from the brush waving a club and shouting a string of Apache words. To assure her that the shots had not been fired carelessly, I rode into the patch

[88]

and, reaching down from the saddle cowboy style, got the bird. I took it over for a view and her scowl changed to a broad grin; the ravens had been damaging her young corn. Jones remarked that the Indian woman would tell everyone the officers at the fort could hit a big crow on the wing.

Riding on to the rendezvous along the East Fork, we did not have a long wait for the carriage. Then taking off our uniforms, we changed into fatigue clothing and knotted the corners of handkerchiefs to use them for head coverings. Private Carpenter pointed to a place up the slope, and said that the opening was just back of the brush. Grabbing armfuls of paraphernalia, we scrambled up the loose shale for the exploration. At the entrance I tied an end of the heavy string securely to a bush. Then I unrolled the twine as we walked into the opening a few steps before having to stoop low to get into a small chamber. Playing our flashlights around the walls, we saw what looked like a camping place. The floor was deep with powdered dirt, and in back was a portion of a stone wall. Some soldiers had recently built a small fire there, and had scattered the remains of their lunch around. A small opening led on, and above the hole were several hieroglyphic figures. Upon close examination the marks appeared to be of recent origin because the indentations were not discolored. Then Jones discovered a distinct fine-line chisel mark. Some trooper had used a steel tool to make the figures, and it was a good job. At least the imitations had deceived us for awhile.

We entered the hole on our stomachs and crawled down a slope of rock slabs. Every twenty feet or so I tied the trailing string to a rock; therefore if it broke, we could readily find the main string. In some places we had easy going in an almost upright position; in others the passageway was plugged by rock slabs, and it was necessary to wriggle through. Resting in a chamber area, Jones brushed off his jacket and pulled out his wrist watch from a shirt pocket. It did not seem possible that we had been crawling for over half an hour, but the watch indicated that we had. Nothing had been found, and we felt certain that none of the colored troopers had ever crawled in this far.

My flashlight showed several low openings on ahead. We decided that each would explore a branch for a short distance and then meet here and crawl out. Jones had been taking his turn leading and had the ball of twine. Cutting the string at the tie-off place to a rock, I wound some into a separate ball, fastened an end to the main line, and proceeded into a small hole. Worming along for some distance, I came to a pocket-like opening under an overhanging slab. The light showed some bones in a corner. Reaching in as far as possible, my fingers got hold of a long bone. It was a thigh bone of a primitive Indian, yellow from age and the dry air of its resting place. I did not like to disturb the remains of these early-day savages, but decided to take the leg bone and parts of the skull, together with the jaw bones, as specimens for some museum. The floor was covered with a couple of inches of powder-dry dust. Lying on my side, I moved the flashlight around and spied an object resembling a twig. A long stretch reached it. It was a hollow reed with a notch cut in one end. Immediately I realized the possibilities of finding other objects in the dirt accumulations on the floor.

The layers of rocks which formed the entrance looked unsafe, so I withdrew far enough to reverse my position and put my feet against them. It was a solid formation, and therefore back into the burial chamber I went. After some squeezing and grunting I got in far enough to reach the end. A careful search and sifting of the dust through my fingers uncovered fibre strands wrapped with a type of thread made from an animal's ligaments. In the same spot was a small bone pendant with a hole drilled through the large end. Further scratching uncovered a piece of skin with a few beads clining to it. A careful search for beads in the dust disclosed that there were many of the small, cylinder-shaped bits, which had been cut from shells and bones. I picked up almost a handful and then quit.

Backing out of the burial chamber was a struggle, for my jacket caught on a rock. But I had enough space to unbutton it and wriggle free. Within a few feet an enlarged space furnished room to turn around, and I headed out. However, the traveling was difficult because one of my arms was burdened with the bones, making it necessary to hunch along in a prone position using my free arm as a lever on the floor. On the way back I saw another passageway, but the string led into the other fork. It was reassuring to know positively the proper route to follow. Back in the lower chamber I found Jones resting. He also had found a burial place, but had only examined the remains. Wanting to take a look, I followed his string into the place. There were several piles of bones on a rock shelf, but I had sufficient specimens for a museum so I withdrew after a good look. The return journey was faster since we merely followed the string without the slow, cautious movements of our entrance. At the opening I cached the candles for possible future use, and we stepped out into the dazzling sunlight.

That evening I told the captain about our exploration of the cave and showed him the specimens obtained. He was amused at my enthusiasm in securing the bones. Then he told us the story about a Captain John G. Bourke, an aide to General Crook, who years before had taken a large number of Apache baskets from a cave up East Fork. The Indians saw the articles at the fort and complained to the commanding officer that the captain had robbed a funeral cache. The baskets full of corn had been put in the secret place a few years before as a type of offering upon the death of a prominent tribesman. In order to pacify the Apaches Captain Bourke gave them presents and returned the baskets to the cave, sealing up the entrance with stones.

"But you are likely safe, Lieutenant," the captain concluded, "there haven't been any tribesmen of your Indians around here for a thousand years or so." Then as an afterthought he warned, "But don't try to locate Bourke's cache of baskets." After Captain Tillson left the post, I did try to find the cave but was never successful. Perhaps the baskets are in the sealed grotto to this day. The relics I had secured were added to my collection, which I housed in a separate room in my quarters that was fixed up as a den.

Jones and I must have gained a reputation among the troopers for wanting anything out of the ordinary with which to amuse ourselves. One day a member of the wagon train brought in a stray lamb for us, and shortly afterwards one of Sharp's ranchhands gave us a goat to keep the lamb company. It was strange that the soldiers at Fort Apache did not care much for pets, but were interested in ours. The only dogs on the post were Indian curs that wandered in with the reservation

Apaches; the scouts' family dogs stayed at the tepee row. Some cats might have been in the homes of the married men, but I never saw any. At Fort Huachuca there seemingly were as many dogs as soldiers, and at the border station of Lochiel the cats almost overran the barracks area. It became necessary at both stations to issue post orders both to insure proper control of pets and to remove strays that lacked a responsible owner.

The lamb did not make much of a pet, but the goat had a definite individuality. He followed me around like a dog and laid under a desk in the quartermaster office while I was working there. However, I finally had to banish him from the office when he was caught chewing up a freshly typed letter. Thereafter he would stretch out on the walk while I worked inside. Occasionally the billy goat put his front feet on the window sill to watch us or would jump up on the narrow window ledge, standing there for ten minutes at a time to gaze inside. For companionship he eventually made friends with the sheep, and they became inseparable.

The funniest thing the billy ever did occurred in front of the post exchange. He was trotting ahead of me jumping at some cowering Indian dogs waiting near the door for their masters. Suddenly the animal broke into a fast gallop, seemingly on the cushions of his hooves and without making a sound. Ahead was a dog slouching along behind a squaw. The goat hit the innocent victim from the rear, throwing it into the legs of the Indian woman. Down went the squaw scattering an armful of packages, with the mongrel underneath yelping as though about to die. The goat left the ground on a high jump over them and sped around the building out of sight. I do not know if the woman realized that the goat was the culprit, but anyway she got her hands on the dog and beat it unmercifully. I helped to gather up the packages, but made no signs as to what had occurred.

Private Haines was the orderly and handyman at the quartermaster building. He practically adopted the goat. Some afternoons the billy would disappear and could not be located in his usual haunts. The first time this happened, he did not appear until after evening mess. I was standing in front of my quarters when I saw Haines coming across the parade ground, leading the goat by a string. He came up to me all smiles and said, "Suh, Lieutenant, here's your goat." I thanked him for his thoughtfulness and gave him a dime to spend at the post exchange. After several repetitions of this maneuver, it was clear to me that the disappearance of the goat had a direct connection with Haines' shortage of spending money. However, he was such a pleasing fellow and did not use his scheme too frequently, so I tolerated the strategy.

One morning before reveille I heard something moving around in my rooms, but from the sound of hooves I assumed that the goat had found a door open and walked in. The steps could be heard coming down the hallway and then near the head of my bed. I did not turn over to see the animal until a nose was shoved into my hair. Then a snort startled me, and raising up I saw a young burro that looked like an overgrown jackrabbit. For several days an old burro and her colt had been grazing around the parade ground, and I recognized the little creature. Jones came into my room at that moment, and I knew that he had played the prank on me. Outside along the picket fence the old burro was gazing at the quarters, so I carried the offspring in my arms over to her, dropping it carefully alongside the anxious beast.

My interest in Indian artifacts led to an interesting acquaintance. This occurred just when the time arrived for the annual pistol range firing by the troop, and Jones took charge of the work. The course was beyond the stables over near the base of the south rimrock. It was within walking distance, but we wanted the horses to get all the training possible near the shooting, so we went there mounted even though the first week was dismounted firing. When the mounted firing started, the interesting features of horsemanship and handling the pistol started. All safety precautions were strictly enforced, because an automatic weapon in the hands of a man mounted on a skittish horse is an ever-present danger.

During the time my platoon was firing mounted, I noticed a civilian talking to the captain. Upon completion, I walked over to the scoring table and was introduced to Dr. Leslie Spier of the American Museum of Natural History in New York City. He was working on the Apache reservation exploring the sites of ancient pueblo ruins, gathering pieces of pottery, and doing some excavation in the refuse heaps. The Department of Anthropology was interested in tracing the movements and settlement of a prehistoric people designated by archaeologists as ancestors of the present-day Zuñis. Previous surveys in Arizona had been completed in the Little Colorado River basin, and the present study was connected with the upper basin of the Salt River. That evening Spier told us about his work. Without written records of these ancient people, the only means of learning about them and tracing their movements, as well as their relationships with other inhabitants, was to compare objects found in pueblo ruins and caves. Most of the specimens discovered were the remains of buried persons, broken pottery, called sherds, tools, ornaments, pieces of wearing apparel, traces of food, and types of dwellings.

Lieutenant Jones asked if these pueblo and cave dwellers were the ancestors of the Apaches. The archaeologist was of the opinion that the present-day Apaches were not connected with these prehistoric races, but perhaps had arrived later from peoples of the Yukon and Mackenzie area of the Arctic Circle country. At least, studies evidenced that the Apache language had strong connections with the Indians of those areas. One current view was that all American Indians were descendants of migrants across the Bering Strait from Asia. Spier impressed us as a practical scientist because all of his statements were based on findings and not on theoretical or fancied ideas. But he always gave an answer to our queries, stating, if information was incomplete, that others did not necessarily agree with him. I showed him the articles we had secured at the cave, and also the ancient stone ax which the Apache boy had traded to me. He was especially interested in the relics from the burial chamber, and upon my offer picked out a number of the specimens for me to ship to the American Museum. Some months afterwards I received a formal acknowledgment which stated: "The American Museum of Natural History has received from Lieutenant Harold B. Wharfield skeletal and archaeological material from Arizona, and gratefully acknowledges this contribution to its collection."

The next afternoon Spier and I rode up East Fork for several miles before stopping on a small mound where I had frequently dismounted for a rest. It was a pleasant spot, giving a nice view of the barren top of Old Baldy and of several Indian farms along the creek. Spier told me that our resting place was on a large pueblo ruin. It was almost unbelievable. Reaching down he picked up a small piece of buff pottery. "Here is a sherd," he said, handing it to me. "There are some around here. See." And more were close by. "Also you can make out the fallen walls of this old dwelling." Everything became clear as he pointed to the outlines of the building. Walking around the area, I found several more pieces of pottery, and could then understand that the layers of rocks were not a natural formation. The chief explanation for my previous lack of observation was likely that I had been looking at the scenery.

One of the most interesting ruins was located nearby across the creek. The fallen walls were partially covered with dirt, and the outline showed an area of some two hundred feet square. Spier said that some members of the American Museum had dug into this pueblo at a previous time, but that he still hoped to make a few finds. I joined him there one afternoon. A reservation Apache and he were digging a trench near a wall, and several adult skeletons had been uncovered. The next day after duty hours I returned to help with the digging. The collected objects were laid out on a piece of canvas. In addition to the remains of the adult ancients were several urns containing burned bones. A square turquoise pendant had been found near the ear of another small skull, which had been partially uncovered in the trench. We spent an hour or more carefully removing the dirt from the remainder of the skeleton. A group of shells from a bracelet were near a wrist. Spier said that the bones were the remains of a child, and the ornaments had been buried with the little body.

There were a number of the pueblo ruins in the vicinity of the fort; that knowledge added to my pleasure in the region. We made a visit to the cave up East Fork. In the chamber at the opening Spier dug down several feet in the floor dirt, finding burned sticks, charcoal, corncobs, squash seeds and piñon nuts. We followed the string, which Jones and I had left in place, back to the burial chambers. I had secured most of the best specimens on the first trip, but a few more were taken. Leslie Spier was in our vicinity for several weeks before leaving for the Verde Valley over in the vicinity of Prescott. Upon his return to New York City, he wrote me: "An infected hand took me out of the Verde and into Cataract Canyon — a tributary of the Grand Canyon, you know, where I lived with the Havasupai Indians. These people live like the Apache but are of a milder temperament. I lived, ate and went into the sweat Lodge every afternoon — the real life. 'How' to you, Jones, and everybody at Fort Apache." Subsequently he sent me a copy of his study entitled *Ruins in the White Mountains, Arizona.** My experiences with Dr. Leslie Spier made me an amateur "digger" at sites of old forts, abandoned miners' cabins, and any place that had the appearance of a former habitation. Hunting with a shovel became as much fun as with a rifle.

* In October of 1961 I corresponded with Dr. Spier, who wrote me at that time: "Yours is a voice from the distant past — and a very nice voice to hear. Naturally I am very pleased that you thought of me after all these years, and pleased that you wanted to record our pleasant contact at Fort Apache in your reminiscences. I recall those days at Fort Apache very vividly . . ., crawling belly-wise into that cave on East Fork with you, and scouting around among ruins in the district. . . ." Leslie Spier was born on December 13, 1893, and received his Doctor of Philosophy in anthropology from Columbia University in 1920. The first of his numerous publications came in 1913, "The Results of an Archaeological Survey of the State of New Jersey," which appeared in *American Anthropology*. He died on December 3, 1961, only shortly after I corresponded with him.

XII

IN COMMAND OF FORT APACHE

LATE ONE AFTERNOON an orderly rushed into the quartermaster office and informed me that Captain Tillson wanted my presence at the Adjutant's building. Delaying only long enough to lock the safe, I hurried to headquarters. Upon my entering the captain's office, he spun around in his chair, jumped up, and handed me a telegram. The message was from Headquarters, Southern Department, at Fort Sam Houston, and transferred him to duty with the 7th Cavalry at Fort Bliss, Texas. He was aglow with enthusiasm, and said to me, "Lieutenant, you are now commanding officer of Fort Apache. I am leaving immediately, stopping for the night at Cooley's."

We shook hands heartily at his good fortune in securing the change of station that he had wanted so long. All of the paperwork was in order. It only took about ten minutes for him to close the troop fund book and indorse it over to me. Then he sprinted for his quarters in a most unmilitary manner. Within a hour he was seated in a buckboard alongside the driver, with his bedding roll tied in the back seat. The team was put into a fast trot along the officers row in the direction of the reservation road out the west gate. That was the last time I saw Captain Tillson during his active military career. Many years afterwards I was passing through San Antonio and phoned him from a hotel, wanting to pay my respects. He gave me the directions to his country home, stating that I would be met at the lane by an automobile. Upon my query if he had given up horses, he replied, "I'll meet you

[97]

mounted so you'll think we're again at Fort Apache." When I arrived at the side road, it was a thrilling sight to see my captain on a thoroughbred, back straight as an arrow and seated in the saddle like the horseman of years before. For me, Colonel John C. F. Tillson, Jr., USA, Retired, epitomizes one of the best of that dwindling group of frontier cavalrymen who carried on faithfully at isolated posts in the Indian country.

I told Mrs. Tillson, who remained behind to pack, that a quartermaster detail would be placed at her disposal for boxing the household goods, and the captain's horses would be shipped upon receipt of instructions. She did not wait for the packing to be completed, but left with the children after a few days. "I want to get back to civilization," was her explanation. "Three years here is long enough for any white woman."

The evening the captain left I told Jones that we would carry on the affairs at the fort without any change. Everything was running smoothly. Our immediate problem, requiring careful attention, was to maintain the existing morale, since the old soldiers would be apprehensive with a young officer in command. Work and responsibility naturally increased for both of us, and week-end tours in the area ceased. Our carefree days were over for the time being. We restricted most of our relaxation to the post. After evening mess we usually practiced jumping various horses over hurdles along one side of the parade ground. The evening was ended by playing a few sets of tennis until dark and then shooting pool for an hour in the amusement hall. This procedure became a regular routine. Jones was a fine companion and cooperated heartily with everything I wanted to do. In turn, I gave heed to his desires and good suggestions in all cases. During the time that I was in command at the fort, and at later periods when we were associated at Fort Huachuca, there was never an instance that I can recall when he did anything to make me impatient. Perhaps we were too busy taking care of our numerous tasks for disagreement. However, I believe it was largely due to the unbounded enthusiasm of the officer, his common sense, and his spirit of loyalty.

Dr. McLeod told us one evening that he had written the Surgeon General in Washington requesting reassignment to a hospital or release from duty. The limited practice at Fort Apache was a detriment to his medical career. He feared the inactivity here would impair his skills, and it was a handicap to advancement in medical knowledge to be isolated. The dentist had been recalled to Fort Huachuca some time before. Captain Tillson had been transferred. It appeared that now the doctor would be the next to leave. To add to the medico's discontent and woes was a bad case of hemorrhoids that would not respond to his self-treatment. For a couple of weeks he had not been able to ride with us. Often we could hear him groaning in his bedroom. Early one Sunday morning he shouted for us to come over. We dashed across the yard, hurdling the picket fence, and ran into his room. He was doubled up, crouched on his hands and knees in bed, and his brow was dripping with sweat. His only relief from pain was his loud cussing that covered the complete range of his extensive Texas vocabulary. "Get that hypo out of my bag!" he demanded. "Give me a shot! Quick! I can't stand this pain!"

We both grabbed the bag from a nearby stand. I finally got it open. But what to do next? Neither Jones nor I had ever seen the inside of a medical bag before. There was a neat array of bottles, instruments, and some metal tubes. We knew nothing about assembling a hypodermic needle or the proper medication to use. Eventually I found a hypodermic syringe and screwed on the largest needle in the kit. Later we learned it was a dull, discarded special-purpose needle being retained until a replacement was received. The next problem was the medication to put in the tube. The doctor kept pointing and mumbling as I shoved various bottles up to his face for identification. Once he touched one, indicated I had the proper tube, but I had sense enough to read the label. It said something about dangerous, or extreme emergency, along with Latin terms. Finally he calmed down enough to pick out the proper container and instructed me to use half a tablet. I reasoned if half was proper, certainly a quarter of a tablet would be less dangerous. The process of dissolving it in liquid has long since escaped my memory, but I do recall that Jones brought in a glass of water. However, the tap water was likely used to quench our patient's thirst.

When everything was ready for use, the medico pointed to his buttocks and commanded weakly, "Jab it in!" There was no slack in the skin. His position, on chest and knees, drew the hide taut as a drum. Besides, I was not going to thrust a big needle straight into the leg and possibly hit a bone or an artery. My knowledge of the use of a needle was limited to seeing typhoid innoculations of a few soldiers ahead of me in the lineup upon joining the service. However, something had to be done. I kept jabbing at an angle, and the dull needle would slide off without penetrating the hide. I was now sweating more than the groaning medico. Motioning to Jones to take a turn, he refused by shaking his head. "Doc, this needle won't puncture your skin," I finally admitted to him.

He quit groaning long enough to growl, "Lift me up so my arm's free, and I'll show you damn cavalrymen how it's done." Jones held him up a little, while I put the syringe into his hand and directed it toward the skin. He took a backhanded stab and the needle barely entered, but a shove moved it in and I pushed down the plunger. In a few minutes the doctor got relief from his pain and sat up in bed. Knowing that something was wrong with the equipment, he asked to see it. A quick look and he grimaced. "What a thing to use on a person. You couldn't shove that dull needle through tissue paper," was his comment.

Within a week another doctor arrived, and Doctor McLeod was on his way to a new assignment at Walter Reed Army Hospital in Washington. The new medico was Doctor J. Lee Borden from Victoria, Texas.* He was past middle age and a small wrinkled-faced individual, but he was one of the most interesting characters I have ever known. He introduced himself to me as "a pill doctor from Texas, newly in

---

* Dr. Joseph Lee Borden was born on March 7, 1864, and graduated from the University of Tennessee with his M.D. in 1894. He located in western Oklahoma where he had a general practice, working as a horse-and-buggy doctor. Subsequently, he moved to Victoria, Texas, where he worked until entering the Army Medical Corps as a first lieutenant during World War I. Following the termination of his war service, he returned to Texas and practiced until 1928, when a lung condition placed him on the Emergency Officer's Retirement List. He died on November 24, 1942, and was buried in the Fort Sam Houston National Cemetery at San Antonio, Texas.

the army for the duration and not one minute longer." But from my observations of his work at Fort Apache he was much more than his picturesque description. Jones and I spent many an interesting evening listening to his tales of life on the frontier of western Oklahoma where he first practiced before locating in Texas. According to his accounts of the early days he, as a young doctor, made professional calls with a "horse-pistol" in a hind pocket and a medical kit under an arm. There was some family relationship with the Borden milk people, and frequently he quipped that there was more money in canned milk than Texas oil.

He had enough energy for a dozen men. One evening he jumped the hurdles with us, hanging onto the pommel of the saddle with both hands and eyes closed tight. "When I'm killed I don't want to see it done," he explained. However, upon our return to the stables, he refused to jump the picket fence, which was our custom. "Getting too old to trust a crow-bait horse," was his terse excuse. Doctor Borden was interested in my hunting experiences with the scouts. Immediately he wanted to go on a trip after turkey. I told him it meant a long horse-back ride and perhaps some hiking, but he was undaunted and borrowed a shotgun from the troop supply room. One Sunday morning Jesse Palmer took us up East Fork to a corn field belonging to his relatives. Turkey had been seen there. Near an end of the patch the Apache scout chased a turkey down a row within shotgun range of the doctor. As the gobbler took wing a shot crumpled it, bringing the big bird tumbling to the ground. It was a proud moment for the hunter and for all of us. Two other turkeys flew into a pine tree and sat there until I shot them through the necks with a rifle. But the most fun was the feat of our guest. Jesse summed up everybody's feelings toward the fiery little doctor: "Apaches like Doctor Borden. He likes Apaches."

The transfers of the officers gave me some concern that the enlisted men might become restless for a similar change of station. At an isolated post the actions of officers and non-commissioned officers frequently set the trend for the other soldiers. Two of the enlisted men of Troop L had returned to duty from the officers candidate school at Leon Springs, Texas, awaiting their prospective officer commissions and assignments. When their orders arrived, it was my pleasure as Summary Court Officer to take their oaths of office. The former Sergeants Howard Fields and Livingston Williams, now second lieutenants in the National Army, left immediately for an eastern military camp. Whatever effect this event had on the sentiment of other soldiers for leaving Fort Apache was somewhat alleviated by the return of Sergeant George Hall. He had previously been commissioned a captain of the National Army, but resigned after serving several months to come back. The sergeant was a soldier of some influence among the troopers. His recitals that infantry work was chiefly marching with heavy packs and digging trenches with little shovels did much to reduce any discontent among the others.

During this transition period we decided to advance the rifle range work to an earlier date. It would give the troop a new interest; furthermore, there were a number of riflemen among the colored soldiers who desired to secure good records. In those times the government offered a monthly pay increase of five dollars for firing expert, three dollars for sharpshooter, and two dollars for marksman. Some of the men had qualified regularly for a number of years. For the initial year of earning any of the grades, a distinctive badge was awarded, and thereafter an engraved bar for attachment to the medal. It was common to see badges on the soldiers' blouses which had two or three, and in a few cases almost a dozen bars attached. The firing range was some two miles from the post and beyond the drill ground, necessitating the serving of noon mess in the field. This arrangement provided extra training in outdoor messing and establishing a picket line for the horses, as well as the use of accompanying army vehicles.

One afternoon during the practice period for rapid fire a jackrabbit jumped up and ran across in front of the targets. It was a most tempting thing to break discipline and take a shot at the running target. But only one young soldier appeared to have fired at the beast as it fled across his target lane. First Sergeant Key was alert for such a breach of discipline, and he gave the private a severe reprimand. The soldier evidently remonstrated too much, because I heard the first sergeant close the disciplinary action by stating, "Hush your big mouth up or I'll take you to the Lieutenant!"

The number of targets was limited, and only about half of a platoon could fire at one time. For several days at the beginning of the practice-firing everyone was interested in watching those on the line. However, as soon as the novelty wore off, most of the non-participants loafed around or found a shady spot to sleep. Lieutenant Jones suggested that the soldiers be kept busy by stunts on horseback. He had been a member of a monkey-drill team at Fort Myer, Virginia, and knew the fundamentals as well as the complicated stunts. We talked it over and decided that the work should be compulsory for a few days. If the practice showed that a number of the men were interested, then it would be changed to a voluntary basis or dropped. When the free troopers were marched to the picket line I could see that there was a lack of enthusiasm. It looked to them as though they would have to drill instead of loafing.

Upon his arrival, Jones unsaddled his horse and had the men stand around in a circle. Then he showed them a few simple stunts. A soldier held the animal's head while he ran up from the rear, touched his hands on the rump, and vaulted to the mounted position. Then placing his hands on the withers, he raised his body and, swinging horizontally above the horse, crossed his legs and came down facing the rear; by the same movement he once more was facing the front. Reversing the exercise, he returned to the rear position and by a quick movement somersaulted off the animal. Immediately many of the soldiers wanted to try the stunt. A dozen or more of the horses were moved into line. Jones emphasized that the animals' heads should be held high and the bridles jiggled a trifle as the trooper approached on the run from the rear — thereby distracting the horse, as well as lessening the blow in case it did kick. He had the men practice only the mounting. Even the old soldiers caught the enthusiasm and all tried the stunt.

I walked back to the firing position, knowing that the talking and occasional laughter at the picket line would likely distract the work. Upon approaching I saw a non-com jump down from the top of a scoring-desk, but I said nothing. His squad was cleaning rifles, so he had not been derelict in supervision even though watching the monkey-drill. When the firing ended for the day, we all hurried to the crowd around the horses. Jones was just finishing up the first lesson. A number of the troopers were proficient in going through the full series of stunts, and all of the men were enjoying the exhibition.

That was the beginning of one of the most interesting activities at the post. On the afternoons when the group practiced, most of the soldiers gathered around the grounds near the quartermaster building. It soon became such a place of interest that if a man was wanted after duty hours he could be found in the crowd at the corral. The fame of the monkey-drill team spread throughout the region. Frequently cowboys rode into the post to watch the events, and reservation Indians were always in the crowd. The most difficult stunts were over the hurdles. A group of three became expert in jumping Roman-style, standing up on two horses. But the most spectacular were teams of four men — two mounted bareback on horses linked together, and two more troopers seated on the riders' shoulders. This squad had three sets. The drill was executed by jumping the hurdles at the canter with one following the other in regulation column order.

The rodeo organization at Springerville sent a representative to the post, asking that the monkey-drill squad appear there. Upon talking over the request with Jones, I considered at first that it would be a good trip for the entire troop, but I decided against it since the end of the fiscal year was approaching. This closing of the government's accounting period required much additional paperwork that could not be postponed. However, plans were made for Jones to take his monkey-drill squad, a drum and bugle corps of four men which he had organized, and the necessary escort wagons around the mountain road to Springerville. Upon returning from the trip, all were delighted with the hospitable reception received from the Mormon town. So enthusiastic were the men that they asked to go through the same program for the benefit of us at the post. Knowing that the others of the troop would like to be a part of the act, I set aside the next morning for jumping the hurdles, followed by the monkey-drill show. Lieutenant Jones told me that the rodeo crowd was actually amazed at the circus-acrobatics on horseback, and, upon request of the chairman, the hurdle events were all repeated. It was as much pleasure to the troopers to be recognized as it was for the spectators to sit and watch.

XIII

CAPTURING A TULAPAI CAMP

OUR ACTIVITIES WERE SO INTERESTING, coupled with the contentment of the troopers, that each day was anticipated with pleasure. The only problem was to do all the things that came to mind. One Sunday morning Sergeant Long and I were working at the quartermaster office closing the accounts for hay and wood which had been purchased from the reservation Apaches on the previous day. It was a short job, and upon completion we sat around for a chat about the post activities. He commented that everything was going too smoothly to last; there must be a "storm brewing" somewhere. I laughed at his pessimism and replied that this time the old soldiers' axiom was wrong.

Leaving the office I wandered over to the scout row to talk with any of them who might be about. It was always a pleasure to spend a few minutes there since the domestic life of these Apaches never ceased to fascinate me. Eskipbygojo was the only one in view, and I stopped to watch him braiding some leather thongs into a quirt. When I asked where the other scouts were, the only answer received was, "Maybe see other friend somewhere." He was usually a talkative man, the one who had most to say about conditions and other people. However, his lack of conversation did not cause any special attention on my part, and I went on. Some of the women looked out of their tepees, but upon seeing me drew back under cover. This was not their usual conduct toward me since we had become acquainted. Even though shy in my presence, they had previously gone about their outside duties freely. Even this change in attitude did not impress itself on my mind.

Near the end of the row one of the scouts rode in front of me and fell off his horse. Getting to his feet he stumbled around, then seeing me approach he tried to salute. I knew at once that he was drunk. Up close the smell of sour corn-liquor from his slopped-up shirt front was proof that he had been at a tulapai camp. The man was one of the most reliable and trustworthy scouts; however, the temptation offered by some tulapai drinking party had been too strong for him to resist. For a moment I thought of telling him to go to his tepee and stay there. He was not disturbing anybody, and furthermore the act of leaving the drinking bout evidenced a sense of responsibility. But the strange actions of the women as well as Eskipbygojo came to my mind. Very likely more scouts were involved. If so, leniency could not be extended to any individual.

I concluded it was necessary to confine the scout until further investigation, so I said, "Tell your woman you are going over to the guardhouse to be locked up." Putting his head inside his tepee, he mumbled something in Apache, then backed out and stumbled down the slope toward the post. Following him over, I told Sergeant Peters of the guard that the scout was under arrest and was to be confined until further orders. A private of the guard told me that the Apache had ridden up from the old sawmill area just a few minutes before. Upon that news I sent the sergeant over to the barracks to inquire if anyone had seen scouts leaving the post during the morning. He returned shortly with the information that a number had been noticed galloping toward a mesa north of the fort.

Telling Sergeant Peters to report to me, mounted, at the Adjutant's building, together with another member of the guard, I hustled over to the stables for my horse. Over at the officers quarters the mount of Lieutenant Jones was tied to the hitching-post, so within a few minutes we were on our way to headquarters. There ahead of us were the members of the guard, and First Sergeant Key was on the run across from the barracks. I told the first sergeant to alert only the platoon sergeants that we were going out to find the tulapai camp. Also, I gave instructions that Medical Lieutenant Borden would be in charge of the post, but the detailed actions for any troop movements would be the first sergeant's responsibility.

Outside the west gate Jones and I loaded our pistols, and Sergeant Peters and the private put clips of shells in their rifles. At the base of the mesa there was a fork in the trail. Fresh pony tracks led around to the west, so Jones and the private took the steep grade toward the top for a possible cover of my movements in following the signs. Along the lower trail Sergeant Peters saw a person riding down a ridge, and my field glasses disclosed that it was an Apache scout. Moving into a draw out of sight, we galloped over to intercept him. In a few minutes our course crossed a rise, and there about fifty yards on ahead was the Apache. I shouted his name and ordered him to stop. Yanking the pony around to retreat, he ducked low in the saddle and spurred the animal into a gallop.

It was high time to stop such disobedience, so I jumped off my mount. Yanking the rifle out of the sergeant's scabbard, and aiming at a dirt bank ahead and above the fleeing scout, I fired. The bullet loosened a cloud of dirt ahead of him, and he changed his course toward a thicket. Next I fired at the opposite side near the brush; the bullet hit a rock and went whistling off into the air. Again he swung his pony away from the trail and toward a sheltering ridge. Two shots into the ground ahead failed to stop his escape, so I quit. He was off some distance by now. Handing the rifle back to the sergeant with an order to fill up the magazine, I received the astounding reply that he had only brought one clip of ammunition. The soldier explained that his arms as sergeant of the guard was a pistol, and the rifle belonged to a private. It was quite an apprehensive situation to have only a pistol for protection and perhaps an aroused Apache to encounter. I did not know the scout too well, for up to a month before he had been one of Peasoup's mule-skinners on the wagon train. Furthermore a drunken Indian is usually like a wild man, an entirely different character from his normal self.

I ordered the sergeant to ride back for his platoon of soldiers, leaving the balance of the troop for duty around the post. I told the sergeant that his return route should be up the trail which Lieutenant Jones had

Wharfield and Dr. Leslie Spier at a pueblo ruin.

The "Cherry-Cow" cowboys outside the Indian Creek corral at the end of a day's work.

After the troops had ridden two of the wild ones, the owner, standing in front of the gate post, looks for one that had never seen a man before.

John Earl, left, and helper.

taken, and once on top he could search around for us. Upon receiving the instructions, he left at a gallop. I decided to go on around toward the other side, not wanting to continue up the trail in the direction taken by the Apache. After going half a mile or so, I reached a point giving me a good view of the lower country. Four or five Indians appeared out on the flat galloping in my direction. Suddenly they stopped and dismounted, one pointing toward me. It was a suspicious action so I jabbed the spurs into my mount, getting in behind some huge boulders. There an old cattle path came out of a thicket, making good cover toward the top. Within a few minutes the ground levelled off, and ahead the brush thinned out.

Just before leaving the thicket, I heard a voice from higher up on a rocky knoll command, "Stay where you are!" It was Lieutenant Jones speaking. I shouted to him. Then I rode out of the trees right into the middle of the tulapai camp. Near a piñon tree was a small brush wickiup with a fire in front. Several five-gallon cans were nearby. Standing alongside of a tree was a scout stuffing leaves into his mouth in an attempt to get rid of the liquor odor. Another sat on the ground, head hanging down and a tin can laying at his feet. Standing around with sullen faces were four reservation Apaches. Several strange squaws were sprawled out near the fire. Staggering around in the brush was a young squaw trying to gather firewood. Two more scouts lay prostrate inside the brush tepee. Jones came down from his rocky perch and joined me. "Heard you shooting down the other side," he commented, "But knew you could take care of yourself, so decided to hold this camp for a little while before looking you up."

Climbing up on a high rock, I peered out across the low lands toward the fort for sight of the troopers. A column of cavalrymen was coming at a gallop toward the mesa. Since the lieutenant had everything under control, I directed the private to hurry down the trail with instructions for Sergeant Peters that only a squad should come up. The scout, who was chewing the leaves, came over to me and saluted. "Lieutenant," he stammered, "I just got here. One of the scout's squaw asked me to get her man." He was a good Apache. His excuses were distressing to me since it was an alibi.

"You are partly drunk right now," was my terse rejoinder. "Did I ever lie to you or any other scout? Don't you lie to me!"

At that he hung his head in shame and meekly said, "You are right, Lieutenant. I'll never lie to you." I walked over and patted him on the shoulder to relieve his humiliation. We had been good friends, and my expression was an assurance that the relationship continued. Much relieved, he spit out the leaves and, walking over to a can of tulapai, kicked it over. Then returning to me, he stood at attention by my side. Again I patted him on the shoulder.

Within ten or fifteen minutes we heard the troop detail approaching. Sergeant Peters arrived first; he had two bandeliers of ammunition crossed over his shoulders and a rifle in hand. Instructions were given to clean out the camp, dump the tulapai, and smash the cans. Then I directed the scout to tell the reservation Apaches that if they ever came into the fort I would put them in the guardhouse. Those who were sober enough understood and asked permission to leave. It was granted, and, picking up their drunken members, they disappeared into the brush. I thought it would be safest for the scouts to walk down the steep trail, and also that the exercise might sober them some. A trooper was placed in charge of each Apache, while others led the ponies. When we arrived back at the fort, there were armed squads posted at various places and a reserve of mounted troopers at the stables. A number of civilians with Winchester rifles were standing on boulders near the west gate. It was not the first time in the history of the post that the troops had been called out to raid a tulapai camp, but those previous actions had concerned reservation Apaches.

That evening I sent a telegram to the Headquarters, Southern Department, reporting the incident:

> Report that two officers and twenty-four enlisted men of Troop L, 10th Cavalry were ordered by First Lieutenant Harold B. Wharfield, 10th Cavalry at Fort Apache, Arizona at 12 o'clock noon on date hereof to proceed to an area approximately one mile north of the post to raid and capture an Apache tulapai intoxicating liquor camp which was occupied by enlisted members of Detachment of Indian Scouts who

were there drinking intoxicating liquor, carousing and drunk. Approximately one hundred fifteen enlisted men of the troop in charge of Medical Officer Borden were posted within Fort Apache for protection of property and civilians. At the drinking camp four enlisted members of Detachment Indian Scouts were arrested for drunkness and the tulapai intoxicating liquor was destroyed. No resistance was encountered. There is no further use of troops necessary. Troops returned to post at 4 o'clock P.M. same date. The accused enlisted scouts will be tried by summary court-martial.

WHARFIELD, Commanding Officer.

The arrested scouts were put in the guardhouse. I gave orders to work them hard each day at cleaning the grounds around the buildings and to use them on the garbage detail. The scout who had escaped from me on the trail appeared at reveille the next morning. He also was confined. Subsequently I learned that he was too scared to stop when the shots started hitting around his pony. Speeding out of the area, the Apache had gone in the direction of the Whiteriver agency and hidden out in an arroyo. After dark, still somewhat in a stupor and deathly sick from over-indulgence, he headed up into the wilderness on Mount Baldy. There he either fell asleep or became unconscious in the saddle, and his pony turned around and started for the post. Upon awakening at daybreak the scout found himself at the outskirts of the post buildings.

The old soldiers' axiom of a "storm brewing" had proven true. No longer was I without worries. Some nights I would wake up wondering how to conclude the tulapai matter. Of course the offenders could be tried, but that would besmirch their records. Dr. Borden suggested that they deserved a court-martial and thirty days confinement. Lieutenant Jones must have been sympathetic toward the scouts, because he expressed views that the decision did not concern a junior officer. One evening I passed the guardhouse. On the ground outside the window of a cell sat an Apache woman holding her papoose while the other children played around with some stones. Standing in the cell looking out through the bars was her husband. I had the answer to my problem. These scouts had been punished enough without a court-martial. That night I slept soundly for the first time in over a week.

The next morning I had the guard bring over one of the prisoners who understood English. Upon entering the headquarters office, I could see that he was frightened. His body was as rigid as a statue. Opening up the court-martial manual, I read to him the 104th Article of War, which provided punishment by the commanding officer for minor offenses in lieu of a court-martial trial. "Do you want troop punishment by me or do you want a summary court trial?" I asked.

"No! No! No!" he exclaimed excitedly. "You good to all scouts. You say what me do!"

When he was told that the troop punishment was the ten days already served, the scout grinned happily. "Me never drink damn tulapai no more," was his solemn statement. Stepping to the door, I handed the guard a memorandum for the release of the prisoner, and instructed him to bring over the others. That was the close of the unhappy affair. All of the scouts shook my hand, and grunted much in satisfaction. There was no change in our friendly relationships. Peasoup, who was close to the scouts, told me that the Apaches were greatly ashamed to have caused trouble. They wanted the lieutenant to forgive them and always remain their white friend.

XIV

THE WILD HORSE CORRAL

DURING THE FOLLOWING WEEK all of my duties seemed drudgery. Hard as I tried to get back my enthusiasm, nothing seemed attractive. I was having a letdown after the difficulties and concern of the previous two weeks, and my pep was gone. Friday night I told Jones to take over the morning inspection. I had decided to go into the Indian Creek country for a couple of days and get a change from post activities. Both the medico and he commented they had noticed that the scouts troubles were depressing me, and a leave was in order. Early the next morning I was on my way, leaving the post near the water reservoir and going through the timber up a steep path to the top of the south rimrock. It was an old Indian trail which I had previously discovered. Captain Tillson had told me that Signal Sergeant Barnes, following the Cibicu fight of 1881, had left the fort by a trail up through the rimrock on his fateful journey to Fort Thomas for help. This was likely the same path because none of the scouts knew of any other route up the barrier. Anyway, my enthusiasm was returning just by thinking about the excitement of the past Apache times.

On top, I could see the prairie country extending for a number of miles toward the Black River canyon. Heading in the vicinity of the old Army telegraph line, I found a fresh wagon track going toward Indian Creek. Horseshoe marks were proof that a cattle round-up was in progress somewhere in the region, and this was the chuck-wagon.

Leaving the route of the vehicle, I wandered around in the country for the balance of the day, stopping frequently just to sit under a tree and loaf. Late in the afternoon a cattle holding-corral out on a flat appeared; it looked like a good camping place for the night, so I turned in that direction.

A number of flocks of wild doves were feeding inside the pole fence. A few well-placed shots from my .22 rifle produced enough birds for a meal. Making camp on the bare ground in a sheltered spot, I waited until sundown before lighting a fire to cook the game. My mouth could almost taste the tender meat while it was frying in the well-greased mess-kit. Suddenly the pan caught on fire, and I yanked it off the supporting rocks. Some of the burning grease splashed onto the back of my right hand. Within a minute the entire burned area had raised into a huge blister. My knowledge of treatment of burns was limited: therefore it seemed best to leave it alone and get back to the fort for medical care.

Using my left hand to saddle-up and pick up the equipment, I mounted and started for the post. By now it was pitch-dark. Guiding on a star, I rode for a couple of miles before coming to a patch of trees. Stopping for a moment I contemplated entering the trackless woods and the chances of finding the trail off the rimrock. Then turning around, I headed back in the direction of the corral, arriving there without much difficulty. I slept soundly, and awoke in the morning with the sun shining in my face. My head was pillowed on the injured hand, and the blister had broken. Luckily it was just a superficial burn.

For breakfast I cooked the doves, and then crawled up on the corral fence to enjoy the scenery and take a smoke. It was pleasant there to gaze around indolently, watch my horse munching on the meal of oats, and enjoy the warm sun. About the time I was ready to jump down off the fence, a cloud of dust appeared out on the prairie and soon the sound of bellowing cattle was heard. Then a cowboy came galloping up, answered my wave of the hand, and took his station near an extended wing of the fence. Within a few minutes the herd started arriving, and a number of riders guided the animals into the corral. It was the Chiricahua cattle outfit gathering unbranded calves and cutting

out steers for the market. I spent the rest of the day there watching
the work and talking to the men. Leaving late in the afternoon, I had
an easy ride back to the fort. Now I was thoroughly refreshed, and the
lure of life on the Apache reservation had revived.

After my return the work at the quartermaster office took my attention for several days, and Lieutenant Jones handled the troop drill.
Letters had to be written for authority to store freight at Holbrook;
promotions to private 1st class for deserving members of the quartermaster detachment were forwarded to the Department Quartermaster;
a number of soldier payroll allotments required changes; maintenance
funds for the caretaker at the closed post of Fort Wingate, New Mexico,
were approved; new authorization had to be secured from Chief of
Forage Branch at Chicago for the purchase of hay at the wagon train
camps; the Q.M. Mechanical Repair Shop No. 304 at Fort Sam Houston
was informed for about the fifth time that motor vehicles were not
used at Fort Apache; and a variety of other matters required attention.

It was at this time Peasoup told me, on a lay-over of the wagon train,
that Signal Corps Corporal Harte in the Holbrook Army telegraph
office was spending his own funds for food expenses. Upon examining
the records, I discovered that his commutation of rations was based on
a 1915 letter from Headquarters, Southern Department, providing for
seventy-five cents a day. The Army telegrapher was a very modest man
and hesitated to complain about the matter to the commanding officer.
In response to my request for information, he wrote:

> "1. Please allow me more funds for Ration money, it being
> impossible to secure a meal in Holbrook for less then fifty
> cents.
> "2. Since my arrival June 14, 1917 I have taken from my
> money $153.00 in order to get three meals a day."

The soldier's reply was used as an enclosure for my letter as Acting
Quartermaster, addressed through me as post commander for approval,
and thence to the Department Quartermaster at Fort Sam Houston,
requesting an increase of the ration allowance to the amount of $1.25
per diem. Within some thirty days further indorsements on the com-

munication approved the amount. I had previously eaten a breakfast of hot cakes, eggs, and coffee at the Chinaman's cafe on Main Street in Holbrook for twenty-five cents, so knew the increased commutation was sufficient.

One afternoon I was using the typewriter at the quartermaster office and having poor success in producing a passable letter. Every error required erasures on the original and three copies. It was most frustrating work. The climax came when the rubber of a pencil tore the almost completed page. Yanking the letter from the machine, I crumpled it up and threw it at the waste basket. Just then a trooper came into the office, and I cut short the desire to express my feelings vocally. "Suh, Lieutenant," he said, "Lieutenant Jones got some cowboys outside the post exchange. He wants to know —"

Before he had completed the message, I had grabbed my hat on the way out of the building, thankful for an excuse to get away. At the near end of the post exchange the lieutenant was talking with two strangers. One man was mounted on a mule and the younger on a shaggy-maned cayuse with a hackamore rope tied around the nose and fastened to a halter for a bridle. They were John Earl and one of his helpers. Earl told me that he was the party rounding-up some of the wild horses for the Whiteriver agency, as well as his own use. The holding-corral was one belonging to the Chiricahua people at a place south of the fort toward Turkey Creek. He asked us to come out there some time and look over the bunch that they had gathered. Lieutenant Jones suggested we move the troop to the place for the next Saturday morning inspection and let the boys ride some of the captured wild ponies. So all of us made definite plans to meet at the corral the following Saturday.

That weekend we took the troop to the wild horse corral, arriving about mid-morning where Earl and some of his men awaited us. Shelter halves were pitched, the horses put on the picket line, and a formal inspection made of the field equipment. The cowboys stood around watching the military inspection which added much to the spirit of the troopers. The cooks had been given an extra large kitchen detail in order to prepare an early noon mess. Everyone was anxious to start the wild horse riding, and there was much banter passed about as to who would make a ride and what troopers would be thrown. None of us spent much time eating, and shortly we were at the corral examining the restless herd. The animals were all thin and gaunt because there was no means of feeding them at this isolated place. The only subsistence in the region was the growing prairie grass. It was not possible to herd these wild animals outside the corral like cattle, because once freed they would have fled from the region. The captured ponies did not look much like the prancing wild band that Chicken and I had seen some months before.

One of the young troopers called out, "Mr. Earl, catch me one that ain't never seen no man before." At that challenge one of the cowboys went into the corral and roped a tall, rangy buckskin. The animal scrambled into the midst of the herd, pulling the man along. Several troopers ran to his help, and it was a tug-of-war to drag the choking horse to the outside. A crowd of soldiers surrounded it, holding onto the ears and the nose while one wrapped a gunny sack around the head for a blinder. Many hands got it saddled and literally tossed the rider on top. Then the bronco was turned loose, but it only went into a few gyrations and bucks before straightening out for a dash toward a clump of trees. Earl had kept the lariat around his saddle horn, and checked the animal after a short run, bringing it back to the corral.

There was now a clamour among the troopers for a chance to ride. They realized that the gaunt animals were not strong enough to buck more than a few jumps. They wanted to distinguish themselves as wild bronco riders. The cowboys were kept busy roping while the troopers saddled up the plunging animals. Sometimes there were three or four bucking horses being ridden at the same time. Once a soldier was hoisted up behind a rider, but it was too much of a load for the pony, and the result was merely a run out on the flat.

Finally the boys had all of the riding they wanted. Then it was that the old supply sergeant went into the corral and roped a two-year-old. A number of cowboys yanked it outside, holding the young animal quiet while the non-com mounted bareback. He made a fine ride, and even the cowboys applauded him. After turning the animal loose in the corral, he walked back to John Earl, and commented, "Used to be a bronc-buster for a Texas outfit in the Pecos country when a kid." The knowledge of that fact and the demonstration of his skill immediately increased his prestige among the young soldiers and all of us. The day had been more of an outing than military routine, but the morale of the troopers was of great importance in this frontier region, so we considered the time well spent.

For some weeks I had been expecting that Headquarters, Tenth Cavalry, would assign a captain for duty at the post. It was not customary to leave a first lieutenant in command of a troop for a long period, especially where the responsibility also involved the command of the fort. The first news of a change came to me in a letter from Captain Pink Armstrong, who was at Fort Huachuca on special duty. An order had been issued assigning a captain to Troop L. Pink had talked to the regimental adjutant, asking for my transfer to his troop. From his own experience he knew it was usually difficult to serve under another officer in a troop which a person had previously commanded. The adjutant was sympathetic insofar as a change was concerned, and he put me on the regiment's quota for the one-month course at the Camp Perry, Ohio, Small Arms Firing School. He also told Pink that upon completion I likely would be assigned to Fort Huachuca.

Within a short time the official mail contained copies of the order for the assignment of the captain and my order for the Camp Perry school. And in the next mail was an order assigning a quartermaster captain to Fort Apache. The date for my departure was close at hand, and I did not want to be delayed by transfers after the arrival of the new officers. I was still in command of Fort Apache, so orders were issued appointing Lieutenant Jones as acting quartermaster. Appropriated government funds and all the inventory were transferred to him. It was during the middle of the month, so he did not have to transact any quartermaster business and could maintain the status quo for transfer to the new quartermaster. The troop fund book was closed, and the indorsement prepared for immediate change over.

On the day before my scheduled departure the new troop commander still had not arrived. He was long overdue. I sent a message to Holbrook advising Corporal Harte of my proposed itinerary along with orders to inform the new officer should he be there. That evening I went over to the scouts tepee row for a last smoke with old Billy C F. We squatted on the ground outside his abode for a longer time than usual. As on previous visits there was no talk since he did not even understand pidgin-English. When I got up to leave the expression on the scout's wrinkled face seemed to bespeak that it was our last time together. Touching my shirt front and then pointing far to the north, I said, "Billy, I go to-morrow."

He knew what I meant; perhaps others had told him about it. Whatever was the source of his comprehension, he shook my hand for a long time, and grunted something in Apache. I hope — and believe — it was that we would always be friends.

The next morning I took the mail stage to Holbrook. There I chanced to meet the new captain who had just arrived by rail. He was most agreeable, and said something to the effect that his travel leave had been over-stayed. At midnight the Santa Fe train stopped upon signal, and I was on my way to Camp Perry. At the close of the school, I received orders assigning me to command Headquarters Troop at Fort Huachuca. I have never gone back to Fort Apache. It has been long abandoned by the War Department, and is now an Indian school.* I always want to remember the old fort as it was in 1918 — the cavalry, the scouts, Peasoup's wagon train, the early-day buildings and stables, the kerosene street-lamps and the boardwalks, old-fashioned picket fences around the quarters, the white-washed adobe Adjutant's building, and just outside the east post proper the long line of Apache scouts' tepees.

---

* Fort Apache and the military reservation was abandoned by the Army in 1922 and transferred to the Department of the Interior. See General Order No. 42, War Department, October 20, 1922. The old fort is now the location of the Theodore Roosevelt School of the Bureau of Indian Affairs; this school is for Apache children from isolated areas and for those without family connections.

INDEX

A

A-48 (Apache Indian), 53

American Museum of Natural History (New York City), 93, 94

A-100 (Apache), camp of, 56-57

Apache Indians, at Cibicu Creek fight, 15; clothing of women, 23-24; numbering system on reservations, 53; Chiricahua Apaches, 2, 3, 30, 35; Coyotero Apaches, enlisted as scouts, 19; Jicarilla Apaches, 8; Mescalero Apaches, 2; Sierra Blanca Apaches, 8, 9; White Mountain Apaches, enlisted as scouts, 3, 19.

Apache Scouts, emblem of, 18n; history of, 19-20; medals won by, 20n; on Pershing Expedition, 20, 20n-21n; letters written by, 20n-21n; enlistment records of, 21-22, 22n; on a manhunt, 55-59; and *passim*

Arivaca (Arizona), 3

Armstrong, Pinckney, noted, 18, 28, 30, 36, 118; Wharfield serves under, 1-3; biographical note on, 2n-3n

Askeldelinny, with General Crook, 23

B

Barnes, Will C., 15, 113

Barton, Robert M., 5

Big Bonita Creek (Arizona), noted, 30; flood at, 37-38.

Billy C F, noted, 87, 119; service record of, 22; on a manhunt, 56-59

Billy Jess, service record of, 22

Bird, L. A., apprehends deserter, 60-61

Black River (Arizona), noted, 9, 28, 72; crossing at, 69-71

Bones, Charles, noted, 64; service record of, 21

Borden, Dr. J. Lee, noted, 108, 111; biographical information on, 100-101, 100n; hunting, 101

Bourke, John G., 91

Bronco Canyon (Arizona), 72

Brelsford, Mrs. Gordon, 39n

C

Cabell, De Rosey C., 2

Camp Perry (Ohio), Wharfield ordered to, 118-119

Carpenter, Private, 66, 74, 89

Cassadore Springs (Arizona), 72

Cataract Canyon (Arizona), 96

Cemetery, Indian, 64-65

Chaplin, Charlie, 59

Chicken (Apache Scout), noted, 23, 25, 65, 117; described, 17-18; on Pershing Expedition, 20; service record of, 21; hunts with Wharfield, 28-38; on a manhunt, 55-59

Chiricahua Cattle Company, noted, 4, 6, 29, 33, 62; round-up of, 114-118

Chissay, service record of, 22

Chow Big, noted, 87; described, 18; service record of, 21; on a manhunt, 56-59

Cibecue (Arizona), 69

Cibicu Creek fight, 15, 70, 113

Civil War, 1, 8

Cochise County (Arizona), 23

Cody, John, noted, 20; service record of, 22

Comanche Indians, 2

Cooley, Bert, 9

Cooley, Corydon Eliphalet, 9-10

Cooley, Molly, noted, 97; Wharfield meets, 8-10

Cooley Ranch, 9-10, 17

Corn Creek (Arizona), 30

Court-martials, 55, 59

Cowart, Corporal, 48

Crook, George, noted, 3, 8, 9, 23, 48, 53, 70, 91; and Apache Scouts, 19

Cuba, 2

D

Dana, James J., 35n

Davis, Britton, commands Apache Scouts, 19

DeKlay, service record of, 22; with General Crook, 23

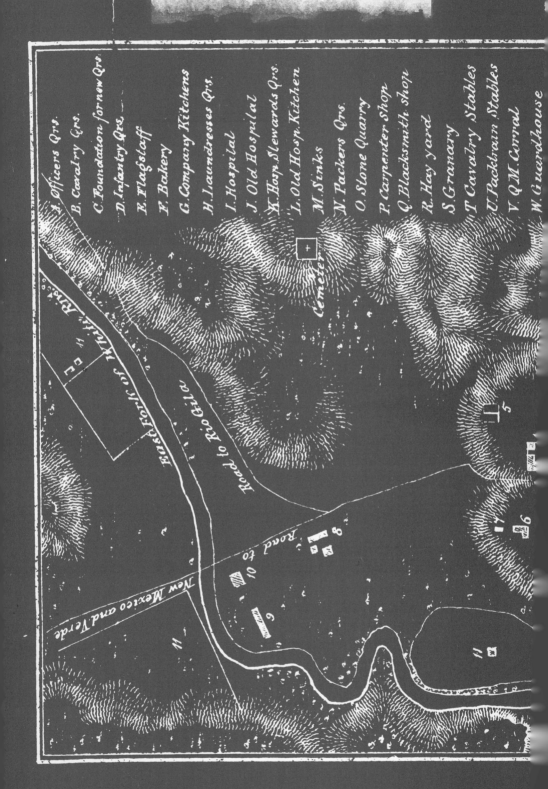

A. Officers Qrs.
B. Cavalry Qrs.
C. Foundation for new Qrs.
D. Infantry Qrs.
E. Flagstaff
F. Bakery
G. Company Kitchens
H. Laundresses Qrs.
I. Hospital
J. Old Hospital
K. Hosp. Stewards Qrs.
L. Old Hosp. Kitchen
M. Sinks
N. Packers Qrs.
O. Stone Quarry
P. Carpenter Shop
Q. Blacksmith Shop
R. Hay yard
S. Granary
T. Cavalry Stables
U. Packtrain Stables
V. QM Corral
W. Guardhouse

Cemetery

East Fork of White River

Road to Rio Gila

New Mexico and Verde

Road to